Dancing Into the Anointing

Touching the Heart of God Through Dance

Aimee Verduzco Kovacs, Ph.D.

Treasure House

An Imprint of

Destiny Image® Publishers, Inc.
P.O. Box 310
Shippensburg, PA 17257-0310

"For where your treasure is,
there will your heart be also." Matthew 6:21

ISBN 1-56043-277-2

For Worldwide Distribution
Printed in the U.S.A.

First Printing: 1996   Second Printing: 1998

This book and all other Destiny Image, Revival Press,
and Treasure House books are available
at Christian bookstores and distributors worldwide.

For a U.S. bookstore nearest you, call **1-800-722-6774**.
For more information on foreign distributors,
call **717-532-3040**.
Or reach us on the Internet: **http://www.reapernet.com**

Therefore they shall come and sing in the height of Zion, and shall flow together to the goodness of the Lord, for wheat, and for wine...and their soul shall be as a watered garden; and they shall not sorrow any more at all. Then shall the virgin rejoice in the dance, both young men and old together: for I will turn their mourning into joy, and will comfort them, and make them rejoice from their sorrow (Jeremiah 31:12-13).

But this I confess unto thee, that after the way which they call heresy, so worship I the God of my fathers, believing all things which are written in the law and in the prophets (Acts 24:14).

Dedication

I dedicate this book to my heavenly Father who always takes excellent care of me; to Jesus Christ who paid the price for me and forever makes intercession for me; and to the precious Holy Spirit who guides me into all truth and who reveals Jesus Christ to me and through me.

To my husband Jim who loves me, takes good care of me, provides for me, and gives me the liberty to work in my Father's vineyard. I love you, Jim!

To my son Brandon who helped me make it through when the times were rough. Without your faith and love I could have never made it, Bro! I love you more than you could ever know.

To an organization that unfortunately no longer exists—Born Again Marriages. Kent and Drew, I owe you thanks for teaching me how to war for my marriage.

To the people in our prayer group who, like David's mighty men, would lay down their lives for me: Gail, Barbara, Carol, Mary Beth, Beverly, Kenny, Lenny, Dan, Robin, Claudette, Janet, Leslie, and all the other friends too numerous to mention.

To Apostle Paul Shields and his wife Gloria for their financial support.

To Attorney Gil Messina for his legal advice.

To my pastor, Bishop Jordan, who opened the door for me to allow God to use the gifts that are in me, and who taught me the wisdom of Solomon; and to his wife who is an example of the virtuous woman.

To my cousin Armi and her husband who prayed me into the Kingdom.

To Pastors Cathie and Bernie Brewster, Jr., for helping publish this book.

To Grace Schlenker for typing this book. She is the best!

To my friends who were always there for me, Joan and Jim, Joan F., Valerie, Eloise, Linda, and Beverly.

To my grandmother who taught me wisdom for living.

And last, but not least, to my father Arturo who loved me and spoiled me as a child, and to my mother Hilaria who sacrificed for me and who brought me up in the ways of God. I wish you were alive to see your grandson and to see what God has done for me. I love you, Mom and Dad.

Contents

Purpose viii

Introduction ix

Chapter 1   Hearing the Call to Dance 1

Chapter 2   The Dancing Bride of Christ 5

Chapter 3   Dance in the Tabernacles of Moses
and David and the Temple of Solomon 21

Chapter 4   Types and Purposes
of Dance in the Church 37

Chapter 5   Flowing Together With the Pastor,
Music Leader, and Dance Leader 67

Chapter 6   How to Start a Dance Team 77

Chapter 7   Technical Aspects of Dance 83

Bibliography 97

About the Author 99

Purpose

The purpose of this book is to unlock scriptural understanding concerning the importance, power, and command of God to dance in the church and at home. This understanding will help to fulfill a portion of Ephesians 4:13, "Till we all come in unity of the faith, and of the knowledge of the Son of God, unto a perfect man, unto the measure of the stature of the fulness of Christ."

Introduction

Nothing is more devastating to the Body of Christ than allowing the devil to divide and conquer. This usually takes place because of a lack of knowledge or is due to not dividing the Word rightly. It breaks my heart to see people like Joseph and Mary looking for room at the inn and finding none. So many today are brokenhearted, discouraged, and confused. There is a call in them to bring glory to God through the talent God has given them, yet they don't know where to go to use this talent. Door after door has been shut in their face. They have been misunderstood, rejected, and even scoffed at for thinking that God could use such a thing as dance in the Church. After all, God is this holy God in Heaven and you have to approach Him with fear and reverence. There is no room for joy or liberty in the Holy Ghost. He is a serious God.

If this is the God you have been serving, I have good news for you. The God of Abraham, Isaac, and Jacob is a fun God who delights in the praises of His people:

But Thou art holy, O Thou that inhabitest the praises of Israel (Psalm 22:3).

And they worshipped Him, and returned to Jerusalem with great joy: and were continually in the temple, praising and blessing God. Amen (Luke 24:52-53).

Praise ye the Lord. Praise God in His sanctuary: praise Him in the firmament of His power. ... Praise Him with the timbrel and dance: praise Him with stringed instruments and organs. Praise Him upon the loud cymbals: praise Him upon the high sounding cymbals (Psalm 150:1,4-5).

For years the Church has been defeated because we have not known how to fight the devil. We have said prayers, not knowing why some were answered and some were not. In this endtime God is showing us the plan. One of the weapons is dance: "Let them praise His name in the dance.... To bind their kings with chains, and their nobles with fetters of iron; to execute upon them the judgment written: this honour have all His saints. Praise ye the Lord" (Ps. 149:3,8-9).

This book has been prepared to take us from praise to worship as we dance before the Lord at home and corporately. We are lively stones (see 1 Pet. 2:5). When we come together to praise God, He invites us into worship as we build Him a spiritual habitation. There is power in agreement. The more of us who gather together in agreement, the greater the anointing. Let us dance into the anointing by having a clear understanding of the place of dance in the Church and at home. Today, God has given us great illumination and insight into His word concerning the dance. Let's use it and put the devil to flight. Let's make the kingdoms of this world into the kingdoms of our God and of His Son Jesus Christ.

This book was ordained of God. The prophetic word of the Lord was spoken concerning the writing of this book by several well-known and well-established prophets of God. It was nine years in the making. The Lord had me attend many conferences on praise and worship, as well as on dance, prophecy, and other related areas. He allowed me to learn through trial and error. God put me on the potter's wheel, molded me, formed me, removed the parts that did not fit His character, and continues to work on me today.

Chapters 1 and 2 of this book will lead the reader through a study of dance as it applies to the Bride of Christ. It will also give insight into the importance of allowing the sacrifice of praise to be fully consumed.

Chapter 3 includes an in-depth study of the Tabernacles of Moses and David and the Temple of Solomon. It will present the place of dance in each one.

Chapter 4 will reveal the purpose of dance and will study each type:
  A. Praise dance
  B. Worship dance
  C. Warfare dance
  D. Celebration dance
  E. Travail dance
  F. Prophetic dance

Other occasions for dance—including ordinations, weddings, baby dedications, funerals, and even evangelistic services—will also be considered in Chapter 4.

Chapter 5 deals with how the dance leader should work and flow together with the music leader, and the pastor.

Chapter 6 explains how to start a dance team and how to lead a dance team.

Chapter 7 includes the technical aspects of dance, such as focus, quality of movement, floor pattern, level, and warm-up exercises.

As we strive to gain a better understanding of the plans and purpose of dance in the church as seen through Scripture, the Holy Spirit will illuminate that which had been hidden in the Word. I pray that this book will cause you to see victory in every area of your life as you apply these principles to your life, and that it will bring unity to the Body of Christ.

Chapter 1

Hearing the Call to Dance

The Spirit of the Lord God is upon me; because the Lord hath anointed me to preach good tidings unto the meek; He hath sent me to bind up the brokenhearted, to proclaim liberty to the captives, and the opening of the prison to them that are bound (Isaiah 61:1).

To appoint unto them that mourn in Zion, to give unto them beauty for ashes, the oil of joy for mourning, the garment of praise for the spirit of heaviness; that they may be called trees of righteousness, the planting of the Lord, that He might be glorified (Isaiah 61:3).

It was October of 1984. I was sitting in a women's conference in Denver, Colorado, praising the Lord. Suddenly, the power of the Holy Spirit fell upon me and I felt an inward voice telling me to get up and dance before the Lord. I said "no" to the inward voice. Surely I could not have heard that from God. *People don't dance in church,* or so I thought. As quickly as I resisted the unction to dance, it went to the person who was playing the drums. He began to play a drum roll that was unrehearsed. The presence of the Holy Spirit filled the coliseum. People were filled with the joy of the Lord and praised God as King David had done when Michal, his wife, got angry at him for dancing before the Lord.

Suddenly the anointing lifted from the drummer and fell upon the lead singer. She started singing a song of the Lord, a spontaneous, unrehearsed song that had never been sung on the earth before.

The Holy Spirit said to me in a still, small voice,"I did that so you would know that it was My anointing you felt when I asked you to dance before Me." Prior to this time, I had not understood what an anointing was. Now I had firsthand knowledge of what an anointing felt like. I said to the Lord, "Forgive me for having grieved the Holy Spirit. Next time You tell me to dance I will obey." From that time on, I set out to learn all I could about the dance through searching the Scriptures.

The first Scripture the Holy Spirit led me to was Psalm 68:25: "The singers went before, the players on instruments followed after; among them were the damsels playing with timbrels." At that point, the Holy Spirit gave me a vision of a circle of women dancing before the Lord. The Holy Spirit then led me to Psalm 149:3: "Let them praise His name in the dance: let them sing praises unto Him with the timbrel and harp."

Well, that settled the matter for me as to whether people are to dance before the Lord or not. That started my quest to understand all I could about God's word concerning dance in the church. Now I had to seek a place of expression, since the church I was a member of did not believe in dancing before the Lord.

The Holy Spirit led me to a conference that was being held in New Jersey, about 45 minutes from where I was living. As I was praising the Lord during this conference, the anointing fell upon me, and the Holy Spirit said, "Get up and praise Me in the dance." I was afraid to disobey the Holy Spirit, but at the same time, I was afraid of being thrown out of the conference. I had never met the pastor before and did not know what his beliefs were concerning the dance. Nevertheless, I decided to fear God rather than man.

I got out of my seat and went to the front of the room. I danced before the Lord in abandonment. The presence of the Lord was so glorious and wonderful I did not care what would happen. I lost sight of the congregation and entered into the Holy of Holies as I danced before the Lord Jesus Christ.

After the service was over, the pastor came up to me and said, "You are it."

"I am what?" I responded.

He said, "The Lord told me He is restoring the arts back to the church to bring Him glory. God said He was going to send me a dancer. He showed me a vision of you doing a circle dance with several other women."

Needless to say, I was in shock. God had shown him the same vision God had shown me! That was the second confirmation I needed to know I had truly heard from God.

This was the beginning of ecstasy as the Lord invited me to enter into His gates with thanksgiving and into His courts with praise. This was also the beginning of sorrows as persecution came because of the lack of understanding in the Body of Christ concerning the place and purpose of dance in the Church.

It is important to realize that our misery prepares us for ministry. Our persecution can either make us bitter or better. I chose to let it make me better. I chose to obey the command of the Lord Jesus Christ to love our enemies and to bless those who say all manner of evil against us. Faith works by love, and love never fails!

Ten years have gone by and the Lord has opened many doors for me to give Him glory through the dance. I have danced and preached the gospel through dance in Jerusalem, at the United Nations, in the ghettos of Chicago, and throughout the United States. I minister with this understanding utmost in my mind, that "in Him I live, and *move*, and have my being" (see Acts 17:28).

Chapter 2

The Dancing Bride of Christ

How important is dance in the overall picture of the Kingdom of God? First Corinthians 15:25 says, "For He must reign, till He hath put all enemies under His feet." And Psalm 110:1 says, "The Lord said unto my Lord, Sit Thou at My right hand, until I make Thine enemies Thy footstool." All power was given to Jesus in Heaven and earth (see Mt. 28:18), and as His body, we now have that power.

How does all this fit in with dance in the Church? Let's go back to Psalm 149:

> Let them praise His name in the **dance**.... Let the **high praises** of God be in their mouth, and a **two-edged sword in their hand; to execute vengeance upon the heathen, and punishments upon the people; to bind their kings with chains, and their nobles with fetters of iron; to execute upon them the judgment written: this honour have all His saints**. Praise ye the Lord (Psalm 149:3,6-9).

There is something that happens in the spirit realm when we dance before the Lord. He uses the foolish things of this world to confound the wise (see 1 Cor. 1:27). We are told in

Scripture to lift up holy hands. We are also told to clap our hands. These actions and other actions of the body bind the kings of satan in the spirit realm. The manifestation of such actions can then be seen in answered prayers as we do warfare through dance. Every kingdom we take back for God— in our families, jobs, business, church—is one more enemy that is made a footstool for Jesus. Thus, the kingdoms of this world become the kingdoms of God and of His Son. We will discuss this topic in more detail when we study the warfare dance in Chapter 4.

At this juncture, I would like to clarify one thing. Dance is not the only thing God is using to establish His Kingdom on earth. Dance is just one small part in the overall scheme of things. It is one small puzzle piece. However, without this piece, the puzzle is incomplete.

To find out where this puzzle piece fits, let's look at First Chronicles 15:25–16:43. This is a description of corporate worship in the Tabernacle of David. The mention of King David wearing fine *linen* garments foreshadows Jesus' finished work at the cross because it is symbolic of being saved by grace and dying to the flesh. Linen and wool can be used as symbols of salvation by grace through faith versus religion by works, which does not save but rather makes the Word of God of none effect and keeps people in bondage. Linen is a thread or cloth made from flax, which was cultivated in Canaan, the promised land (see Josh. 2:6). "In general, linen was used for all types of clothing, sacking, wrapping for the dead, sails, and curtains. Linen garments were cooler than woolens and especially desirable in hot weather" (*Wycliffe Bible Encyclopedia*, vol. 2). White linen is representative of salvation in that we do not have to work or sweat to get saved; salvation is by grace through faith in the finished work of the cross of Jesus Christ. In contrast, wool garments cause people to sweat if worn in warm weather, thus wool is symbolic of using works to get saved. Also, the fact that linen is used to wrap the dead represents that we have died to ourselves and we have risen in Christ (see Col. 2:12-13), so we have liberty because His yoke is easy and His burden is light (see Mt. 11:30).

Looking again at First Chronicles 15:25–16:43, we find the tabernacle officials corporately praising God with joy and excitement: "Thus all Israel brought up the ark of the covenant of the Lord with shouting, and with sound of the cornet, and with trumpets, and with cymbals, making a noise with psalteries and harps" (1 Chron. 15:28). If David were alive today, many churches would respond like David's wife Michal and despise him for being hilariously happy about the things of God. David was so in love with the Lord that it did not matter what people thought of him. He danced before the Lord with abandonment.

In chapter 16, we see the first order of the service was to offer burnt sacrifices. Scripture tells us in the Book of Revelation that the burnt offering is the prayers and praise of the saints (see Rev. 8:3-4), and this is where dance fits in. Scripture tells us to enter into His gates with thanksgiving and into His court with praise (see Ps. 100:4), for God inhabits the praises of His people (see Ps. 22:3). This is the most powerful way to get into the presence of God.

Each of us is a spirit that has a soul and lives in a body. It is for this reason that we cannot keep the body from expressing the excitement of being in the presence of God. As we feel the manifestation of God's anointing, the body responds to it with movement because it is difficult to contain the holy anointing of God when He chooses to overwhelm us with His presence. It is like an electric current seeking an outlet. Trying to contain it would be like putting a finger in a dam to stop the flow of the water. We will study this in greater detail in Chapter 4 in the section on the prophetic dance.

After offering burnt sacrifices, the second thing David did was to offer peace offerings to God. These peace offerings foreshadowed Jesus, the ultimate peace offering, who would later come to make peace between God and man through His atoning death at the cross.

Third, David blessed the people in the name of the Lord. We see this similar order followed by King Solomon in First Kings 8. During this portion of the service, he preached. He expounded upon God's promises and God's exploits on behalf of His people. In First Kings 8:28-61, Solomon prayed for the people and asked God to forgive those who had sinned. This was a foreshadowing of Jesus' ministry as our intercessor at the right hand of the Father. The fervent prayers of a righteous person availeth much (see Jas. 5:16). So, pastors must intercede for their flock, since they represent the Chief Shepherd and Priest, Jesus Christ, here on earth.

The fourth order of service in the congregation was communion: "And he dealt to every one of Israel, both man and woman, to every one a loaf of bread, and a good piece of flesh, and a flagon of wine" (1 Chron. 16:3).

Fifth, David appointed certain of the Levites to minister before the ark of the Lord, "...and to record, and to thank and praise the Lord God of Israel" (1 Chron. 16:4). This is the time when God invited the congregation to worship Him as He responded to their adoration. Prophecy was released at this time and the recorder recorded what God had to say. This is the time prophecy could come forth through the praise and worship dance team. It is not limited to the dance team. God could use anyone. Since we are attempting to see where the dance fits in corporate worship, this is presented at this point for insight into the place of dance during corporate worship.

The purpose for recording was to remind the king of God's instruction concerning future events. This topic, and the topic on the circle of praise, will be looked at in greater detail in the prophetic chapter of this book. For now, it is sufficient to say that the last portion of the service concluded with the manifested presence of God in the midst of the congregation speaking to them and ministering to their needs.

David concluded the service by offering thanks to God. When the service was over, he left Asaph and his brethren to minister before the ark continually, as every day's work required (see 1 Chron. 16:40). "And all the people departed every man to his house: and David returned to bless his house" (1 Chron. 16:43).

In the church today, the dance may be a new experience to some, but in King David's time, it was an integral part of the service. Upon studying the Scriptures, we find that David offered a sacrifice to God by praying and lifting up holy hands, which is a body movement. Psalm 141:2 gives an account of this, "Let my prayer be set forth before Thee as incense; and the lifting up of my hands as the evening sacrifice."

In considering dance as a part of the church service, one needs to understand that for every counterfeit, there is an original. The devil is not able to create anything original. All he does is copy from God. Just as we have worldly music that does not glorify God, so we have godly music that extols God. In the same way we have dances that incite lust, as in Herodias' daughter (see Mt. 14:6), and we have dances that glorify God, as in Psalm 150:4, "Praise Him with the timbrel and the dance: praise Him with stringed instruments and organs." Praise the Lord that He has turned our mourning into dancing! (See Psalm 30:11.)

How does one distinguish between the dance of the world and the dance that is holy unto God? It is simple. The dance of the world seeks to fulfill the lusts of the person dancing. It is done for self-fulfillment, to seduce or attract attention to self. It is not always bad. It just does not place emphasis on God. There are dances of the world that are not evil in themselves, but they do not point to God. Examples of such dances are folk dances, ballet, line dances, and the like. What makes a dance unacceptable before God is costumes that are skimpy and incite lust, music with words that are anti-Christ, movements of the hips, chest, or pelvis that are seductive or sexually provocative. Any dance that would cause one to sin is not of God.

On the other hand, dance that is pleasing to God is Christ-centered. Examples of dances that God desires for His Church are: praise dance, worship dance, warfare dance, dance of celebration, dance of travail, dance of triumph, prophetic dance, evangelistic dance, and dance to prepare the hearts of the people to hear and receive the preached word of God.

In the following chapters we will take a closer look at each of the dances mentioned above. For now, let us take a look at the actual definition of dance.

The *Wycliffe Bible Encyclopedia*, in its last paragraph on the dance, states, "Dancing in the Bible, except for the daughter of Herodias, seems to have little relationship to the sensual, but rather is associated ordinarily with joy, either because of circumstances or because of gratitude for the Lord's blessings." Wycliffe further states that English words concerning dance in one form or another occur 25 to 30 times in Scripture. The words that are translated in English as whirl, writhe, spring, skip, and revolve are all Hebrew words for dance according to Wycliffe.

The King James Open Bible defines *dance* as an emotional movement of the body. It states that dancing is designed to express joy as in Psalm 30:11a, "Thou hast turned for me my mourning into dancing." Another example given is Luke 15:23-25, where the father celebrated the return of the prodigal son with food, music, and dancing. Still another example given is that of First Samuel 18:6-7:

> *And it came to pass as they came, when David was returned from the slaughter of the Philistine, that the women came out of all cities of Israel, singing and dancing, to meet king Saul, with tabrets, with joy, and with instruments of musick. And the women answered one another as they played, and said, Saul hath slain his thousands, and David his ten thousands.*

This was a prophetic dance. David had not yet slain his ten thousands. This prophetic dance was one of the reasons Saul persecuted David. When he heard of David being praised above him, jealousy entered into Saul's heart. He tried to stop God's prophetic word, but who can win over God's plan?

God is going to have an end-time Church who, like David, will be a people after God's own heart, a people who fear God rather than men, a people who will, like Joshua, march (a form of dance) around the walls of opposition and shout down the walls.

Since the charismatic renewal, which reached its peak in the late 1970's, we have seen the Faith Movement, the Word Movement, and the Kingdom Movement, and we are now in the middle of the Warfare Movement. The Warfare Movement is when, as it says in Matthew 11:12, "...the kingdom of heaven suffereth violence, and the violent take it by force." The force we are talking about is not physical force, but rather, anointing power—the spiritual power that comes as we keep our eyes on Jesus and remember how great He is. As we meditate on the great exploits He has done for us, we will forget our sorrows, fears, doubts, and prejudices and will enter into the joy of the Lord. It will cause our spirit, soul, and body to explode with thanksgiving. We will begin to leap, turn, jump, and shout for joy. We will plug into our spiritual electrical outlet. Our being will become like a lighthouse guiding the lost to salvation, thus preventing their ships from hitting the rocks and crashing.

I believe the last movement of God will be that of Bridehood. Bridehood will encompass all the previous moves of God, as well as the restoration of the fivefold ministry in each local church. Only then will we have unity that will lead to anointings like those of the Day of Pentecost. The unity will not be due to our *cooperation* with one another, but it will be due to our *complementation*. This will not be easy because it will require death to self. Everyone in the local church will have to come to the point where they recognize anointings, giftings, calls of God, and limitations, and will be forced to connect in order to fulfill God's call. Networking will be the key.

Worship, I believe, will be one of the major visible signs of Bridehood. It will be greatly emphasized because Jesus wants to be seen by the world through His Church before the world sees Him face to face.

The understanding of Bridehood will coincide with the final revelation of the glory of God. I believe First Corinthians 13:4-8 describes all the moves of God put together. It is a perfect picture of Bridehood. It requires *faith* to bear all things and believe all things (13:7). It takes the spiritual forces of righteousness, peace, and joy—*Kingdom*—to endure suffering and to be kind and humble (13:4). *Warfare* is required to stand your ground in defense (13:7). It takes *praise* to rejoice not in iniquity, but to rejoice in the truth (13:6). It takes God inhabiting our praises and inviting us to worship to bring down the anointing that destroys all yokes.

"Love never fails" (1 Cor. 13:8a NIV) is going to be the catchphrase of Bridehood. Since faith works by love, we will have no choice but to love and forgive if we are going to overcome the attacks of the enemy.

Because of love, a Bridegroom defends His Bride. Because of love, a Bride has faith in her Bridegroom to provide all her needs. Because of love, a Bride wants to keep her house clean and beautiful to welcome her Bridegroom home to a house with a solid foundation. Because of love, a Bride submits to her Bridegroom's headship. Because of love, she adores her Bridegroom and praises Him for His attributes. Because of love, the Bridegroom responds by blessing His Bride with all the comforts she needs—righteousness, peace, joy—which is the *Kingdom* of God. Because of love, they rejoice together and dance in celebration of their covenant.

Their dance is one of exuberance. It is a dance where all the excitement of the relationship reaches a climax. At that point, the dance begins to slow down to one of worship. The Bridegroom begins to speak to His Bride prophetically, sharing the desires of His heart for His Bride. He gives her direction and instructions. He reveals His love for her. In response to His love, the Bride bows before the Bridegroom in expression of her love. Her high esteem pays homage and veneration to her Bridegroom.

The above scenario of the Bridegroom and the Bride is a description of what should take place in our lives daily before the Lord as we praise and worship Him. It is a description of what should take place in our praise and worship services on Sundays and any time the saints gather together in the sanctuary. Churches that strive to have this love relationship with the Lord during every service will see the glory of God in degrees they have not yet experienced. It is a circle of praise and worship that will release the prophetic word of God, healing, deliverance, salvation, and breakthroughs. God inhabits the praises of His people. He will reveal Himself to us more and more as we learn to praise Him. He will then invite us into worship. Signs and wonders will follow His Word to the degree we are connected to Him by a daily life of fellowship. As we draw near to Him, He will draw near to us.

One of the hindrances I have observed in some churches where I have been invited to minister, is the lack of understanding concerning the praise and worship part of the service. Some praise and worship leaders don't know how to allow the Holy Spirit to lead the service. They have a prearranged order of songs and don't allow the Holy Spirit to move in when He wants to take over. Yes, we are to do things decently and in order. Yes, we start out by faith with a prepared order, but then we have to be sensitive to the Holy Spirit and allow Him to interrupt our plans.

We also have to allow the sacrifice of praise to be totally consumed. I have been to churches where God was about to move into a supernatural dimension of the manifestation of the gifts of the Holy Spirit but because the choir sang the last song in the order of the preplanned service, the announcer came up and started reading the announcements. Those members of the church who were in tune with the Holy Spirit

were left hanging, frustrated, knowing they ﹜
God's manifestation in their midst because of ignc.
the part of the music leader, the pastor, and the annc.

Many church members and some pastors come in la .o
the service because to them the praise and worship part of
the service is to give people time to come in late. If they only
knew that God often does more during that time than during the preaching part of the service, they would see greater
manifestations of the presence of God in their midst.

We need to understand that God desires us to praise
Him so He can invite us to worship. Praise is what we do and
worship is God responding to our praise. We cannot enter
into worship unless God invites us in. He desires to walk
with us and talk with us as He did with Adam and Eve in the
Garden of Eden. Jesus died and was resurrected to restore
this fellowship with His children.

It is true that He talks to us through the written Word
and through the preaching of His Word, but when we gather
together corporately, He desires to manifest Himself to us.
He desires for all the lively stones (see 1 Pet. 2:5) to come together and corporately form a temple not built with human
hands that He can inhabit. In that temple, He desires a platform from which He can speak to His sons and daughters.
He wants to encourage us, edify us, and give us direction
and correction if necessary until we all come together in
unity of the faith. He wants our praise and worship to reach
a climax so He can impregnate us with seeds of greatness.
He wants us to give birth to the fulfillment of all His promises by giving us a vision of His great omnipotent power. He
wants His word to become more real to us than what our circumstances are saying.

His word is the substance of faith. His word does not return to Him void. He always sends His word to bring life

where death existed. He wants us to be a testimony to the world of His love, grace, mercy, and power. He wants us to be living epistles read by men. Many times we miss out on God's greatest miracles because we have a microwave mentality. If our answer doesn't come in 30 seconds, we quit. We say God can't do the same miracles He did of old. We accept defeat, sickness, poverty, death, divorce, and failure because we have bought the lie of the devil through the Pharisees of our time.

Jesus already did all He is going to do. We are His body here on earth left to establish His Kingdom. Mark 16:16-18 says:

> *He that believeth and is baptized shall be saved; but he that believeth not shall be damned. And these signs shall follow them that believe; In My name shall they cast out devils; they shall speak with new tongues; they shall take up serpents; and if they drink any deadly thing, it shall not hurt them; they shall lay hands on the sick, and they shall recover.*

Notice, this did not say it would pass away after the original 12 apostles passed away. It said this sign would follow them that believe! Thank God I am one of them who believe and so are you. God is no respecter of persons. He healed me from a breast tumor, and from hypoglycemia. He healed my marriage after a 15-month separation, did a $10,000 miracle, and performed many other miracles too numerous to mention. If He did it for me, He will do it for you. All it takes is faith, patience, unconditional love, forgiveness, and willingness to be a disciple. You have to be willing like Abraham to sacrifice your Isaac and God will provide a ram in the bush for you.

As we gain a better understanding of the many facets of God's personality and as we gain a deeper understanding of the purpose of praise and worship, we will see greater signs and wonders in our church services, as well as individually at home.

In the Old Testament, God told Moses that the sacrifice the High Priests offered was to be fully consumed. Only after the High Priest performed all the duties in the Outer Court and in the Inner Court could he then enter the Most Holy Place. Likewise today, only as we allow the sacrifice of praise to be fully consumed will God give us the privilege of entering into worship. Yes, we are told in Scripture that we may boldly enter into the Holy of Holies because of Jesus' shed blood. Yes, we know that God is always present with us; however, we also know that we don't always experience the manifestation of the presence of God. This is the issue I am dealing with in this section of the book.

Praise is the sacrifice we offer unto God. It is called a sacrifice because sometimes it is the last thing on earth we feel like doing. Yet praise is covenantal. We don't praise or decide not to praise based on feelings. We praise based on our covenant with God that He will be our God and we will be His people. As His people, we have to obey His Word, which says:

> *Praise ye the Lord. Praise God in His sanctuary.... . Praise Him for His mighty acts: Praise Him according to His excellent greatness. ... Praise Him with the timbrel and dance: Praise Him with stringed instruments and organs. ... Let every thing that hath breath praise the Lord...* (Psalm 150:1-2,4,6).

Praise is the key of David that unlocks all other areas of ministry. The church was a praising church before it was a praying church. This account can be found in Luke 24:51-52, "And it came to pass, while He blessed them, He was parted from them, and carried up into heaven. And they worshipped Him, and returned to Jerusalem with great joy: and were continually in the temple, praising and blessing God. Amen."

The disciples were in the Upper Room for a ten-day praise service. As they praised God, He invited them into worship, which was the manifested presence of God as He poured out His Spirit upon them. Worship, then, is God accepting our praise and inviting us into worship by manifesting His presence in the midst of us. We cannot enter into worship on our own. We must be invited by God. It is the key to discovering and experiencing God.

Worship is throne-centered. It embraces the whole person. A lukewarm heart and a rebellious heart cannot enter into worship. That is why praise is needed first—to allow God to deal with our hard hearts, and with our fears, worries, etc. It prepares our hearts and deals with issues in our lives that block us from the manifested presence of God. It gets our flesh out of the way and leads us to focus on God instead of on self. As we lose sight of self and focus on God, He invites us into worship. Pure hands and a clean heart will enter into an awakening, an awareness of the nearness to God. Dance, if called forth by God at that time, will be one of numerous responses, depending on how God wants to express Himself. The worship dance is not a performance, rather, it is a spontaneous response to the love the creator has for us. "For in Him we live, and move, and have our being" (Acts 17:28a).

God's *Kingdom* comes on earth as it is in Heaven to the degree God's *will* is done on earth as it is in Heaven. The predominant activity in Heaven is worship, as found in the Book of Revelation:

> *And after these things I heard a great voice of much people in heaven, saying, Alleluia; Salvation, and glory, and honour,*

and power, unto the Lord our God. ... And the four and twenty elders and the four beasts fell down and worshipped God that sat on the throne, saying, Amen; Alleluia. ... Let us be glad and rejoice, and give honour to Him: for the marriage of the Lamb is come, and His wife hath made herself ready. And to her was granted that she should be arrayed in fine linen, clean and white: for the fine linen is the righteousness of saints (Revelation 19:1,4,7).

The Jewish faith was centered around the Temple in Jerusalem. Jesus spoke to the woman at the well and told her the day was coming when it would not be important *where* the Jews worshiped but, rather, *how* they worshiped—in spirit and in truth. The truth is that if we are saved, the temple of God is in our hearts. When we come together as lively stones, we form a tabernacle for God to inhabit. "Behold, the tabernacle of God is with men" (Rev. 21:3).

The Book of Revelation is about emptying the heavens and filling the earth with the knowledge of God. God wants to reveal His glory to the earth through us, the sons and daughters of God. God wants the earth to sense His power and His presence through us, the anointed ones (*Christ* means the anointed one). If we are the Body of Christ then we are His anointed ones on the earth. We are His hands to heal, to war, to work, and to help feed the poor, sick, and needy. We are His feet to carry the gospel, to dance in celebration, to dance in travail, to dance in warfare, to preach the gospel through dance. We are His mouth to praise, to preach, to prophecy, to worship, to intercede, and to declare God's good news. We are His ears to hear. We are His eyes to see. We are His heartbeat on the earth. We are messengers of hope, salvation, deliverance, healing, prosperity, peace, and rest in the Lord, and we are a source of joy to the hopeless.

Chapter 3

Dance in the Tabernacles of Moses and David and the Temple of Solomon

After this I will return, and will build again the tabernacle of David, which is fallen down; and I will build again the ruins thereof, and I will set it up: that the residue of men might seek after the Lord, and all the Gentiles, upon whom My name is called, saith the Lord, who doeth all these things (Acts 15:16-17).

In order to understand the importance of praise and worship, we need to understand the three institutions of God throughout history: the Tabernacle of Moses, the Tabernacle of David, and the Temple of Solomon. A complete study of the Tabernacle of Moses, the Tabernacle of David, and the Temple of Solomon would be a book in itself. Therefore, only the most elementary items will be covered in this book as they relate to a better understanding of the place of dance in the Church today.

The Tabernacle of Moses consisted of three places—the Outer Court, the Holy Place, and the Holy of Holies. (See Exodus 25–31.) The Outer Court contained the Brazen Altar and the Brazen Laver. The Brazen Altar was used to offer blood sacrifices for the atonement of sin. This foreshadowed the blood of Jesus shed at the cross to atone for our sins once and for all. Thus, when we become born again by asking Jesus to come live in our heart and to be Lord of our life, and by confessing our sins and repenting of our wicked ways, our sins are forgiven and God remembers them no more. We become new creations in Christ and are now sitting in heavenly places with Christ, as Jesus is the head of the Body, which is His Church (see Eph. 2:6).

The second article found in the Outer Court was the Brazen Laver, where the priests washed their hands and feet before they went into the sanctuary to minister unto the Lord. It was made of looking glasses of the women of Israel, and it represents our cleansing ourselves by the washing of the water of the Word through the teaching of the Holy Spirit (see Jn. 14:26; Eph. 5:26). It is the getting rid of worldly wisdom and renewing our mind with the Word of God, which is the entire Bible. Reading only portions of the Bible without having read the whole thing is what leads people into error and cults. Taken out of context, the Bible can say anything one wants it to say, thus the many religions of the world.

2. The Holy Place is the second division of the Tabernacle of Moses. In it were three articles of furniture. On the north side was the Table of Shewbread. It contained the bread for the priests. It was arranged in two rows of six. This represented the 12 tribes of Israel (see Ex. 28:10-12), the Church (see 1 Cor. 10:17), and Christ as the bread of life (see Jn. 6:48).

On the south side of the Holy Place was the Golden Candlestick, which was made of pure gold and fashioned according to divine design. It had seven branches with seven lamps on the branches. These lamps were filled with oil and burned continually before the Lord. According to Revelation 1:13-20, Jesus is the stem of the seven candles, which represent the seven churches. This Golden Candlestick was the only light in the Holy Place, symbolizing Jesus as the light of the world. The oil of the Golden Candlestick is representative of the Holy Spirit who is depicted in many verses of Scripture as oil or anointing (see 1 Jn. 2:20,27).

The Golden Altar of Incense, the third article found in the Holy Place, was made according to the divine pattern given to Moses by God. It stood in front of the veil that divided the Most Holy Place from the Holy Place. The sanctuary was filled with the fragrance of the spices representing the intercession, worship, and prayers of the people. "By Him therefore let us offer the sacrifice of praise to God continually, that is, the fruit of our lips giving thanks to His name" (Heb. 13:15).

When Jesus died on the cross, the veil that separated the Holy Place from the Most Holy Place was torn. Now we can enter the Most Holy Place boldly. However, many people never or seldom enter the Holy of Holies because they live a "soulish" life. That is to say, their mind is not renewed with the Word of God so they cannot prosper in their relationship with God because they do not feel worthy. "Beloved, I wish above all things that thou mayest prosper and be in health, even as thy soul prospereth" (3 Jn. 2). Since we are a spirit that lives in a body and has a soul (mind, will, intellect, emotions), we need to bypass the soulish thinking to ascend to the higher laws of God that operate in the spirit realm where the battle between the forces of darkness and the hosts of God operate. (Ephesians 6:12-13 says: "For we wrestle not against flesh and blood, but against principalities, against powers, against the rulers of the darkness of this world, against spiritual wickedness in high places. Wherefore take unto you the whole armour of God....") This is not to say that our body does not play a part in praise, but rather that as we offer the sacrifice of praise as an incense to God, He accepts our sacrifice by inviting us into the Holy of Holies as He inhabits the praises of His people (see Ps. 22:3).

Praise ye the Lord. Praise God in His sanctuary: praise Him in the firmament of His power. Praise Him for His mighty acts: praise Him according to His excellent greatness. ... Praise Him with the timbrel and the dance: Praise Him with stringed instruments and organs. Praise Him upon the loud cymbals.... Let every thing that hath breath praise the Lord. Praise ye the Lord (Psalm 150:1-2,4-6).

The Most Holy Place filled the third section of the Tabernacle. The only article of furniture found in this compartment of the Tabernacle was the Ark of the Covenant, a box containing the golden pot of manna, the tablets of the law, and the rod of Aaron that budded. Manna represented that Jesus is the bread of life, the Word of God is our daily manna, and God is our daily provider. The tablets of the law represented the law that God today has written in our heart. The rod of Aaron represented God's election and was symbolic of Jesus Christ the Messiah, the anointed one. The Ark of the Covenant represented the humanity of Jesus Christ (made of acacia wood); the divinity of Christ (overlaid within and without with gold); and the kingship of Jesus (the crown of gold on top). The Mercy Seat, made of solid gold, covered the Ark of the Covenant. It represented that mercy triumphs over judgment because Jesus intercedes for us to the Father by sprinkling His blood over the Mercy Seat. When we sin, He reminds the Father that He has paid the price for us by the shedding of His blood. Cherubim sat on each end of the Mercy Seat with outstretched wings guarding the holiness of the Mercy Seat (Ex. 25:10-22).

It was in this article that the visible glory of God or the presence of God dwelt. If anyone other than the high priest went into the Most Holy Place, they would die. Even the high priest could only go in once a year to sprinkle the Mercy Seat with blood on the Day of Atonement, and even the high priest could die if he went in improperly. Thus, they used to tie bells on him along with a cord to pull him out in case he hadn't followed the proper way to enter into God's presence.

God was and is a God of order. He was very specific with the details He gave Moses for establishing the Tabernacle. God will not tolerate being misrepresented. Moses was unable to enter the promised land because he misrepresented God by having struck the rock twice in anger. God had told him to strike it once. The rock represented Jesus Christ who would die once for our sins. So, the Tabernacle of Moses foreshadowed the coming Messiah.

Jesus was the sacrificial lamb that was slain for our sins. He was the atonement for our sins. In the Tabernacle of Moses, only the high priest could go into the Most Holy Place to be in the presence of God. Today, Jesus is the high priest who sits at the right hand of the Father making intercession for us. Because of Him, we can now go directly into the Most Holy Place to speak to the Father.

Whereas the Tabernacle of Moses represented the law, the Tabernacle of David represents the dispensation of grace in which we now live. For the purpose of understanding praise and worship during this dispensation of grace that we now live in, the two tabernacles will be compared.

In the Tabernacle of Moses, there were no singers until David's time. There were no instruments, and only the high priest ministered before the Ark. There was no giving of thanks, no praise, no psalm singing, no rejoicing, no hand clapping, no shouting, and no dancing (except for Exodus 15 and Joshua 6). The offering of incense was a burning of spices, specified by God, which released a fragrance. The fragrance God is interested in today is our praise that rises up as incense unto God as it did in King David's time.

In contrast to the order of worship in the Tabernacle of Moses, we find the Tabernacle of David totally different. In the Tabernacle of David, there were appointed singers, instruments of music (see 1 Chron. 15:16), giving of thanks, praise, psalm singing, rejoicing, clapping of hands, shouting, dancing, lifting up hands, bowing, seeking the Lord, spiritual sacrifices offered and blessings given.

The writer of Hebrews tells us that we are to come to Mt. Zion and the Tabernacle of David, not to Mt. Sinai and the Tabernacle of Moses under the law. This is not to say that people did not sing or dance during the dispensation of the law. Miriam danced in Exodus 15:20, and Moses sang in thanksgiving for victory in crossing the Red Sea. However, both of these instances occurred outside the Tabernacle.

In contrast to the Tabernacle of Moses, David established the order of worship given to him by God as a pattern to be followed in the Tabernacle of David. Prior to receiving God's pattern, David had moved the Ark according to what was right in his own eyes, and he learned a lesson he would never forget. Because he did not follow God's pattern, the Ark brought curses instead of bringing blessings. Fear came upon David and he took the Ark not to the City of David but rather to the house of Obededom where it stayed for three months (see 1 Chron. 13:1-14). In First Chronicles 15, we read that David realized he had made a mistake; after seeking God's direction, he took the Ark to the City of David and established the Tabernacle of David according to God's pattern.

As we study the Tabernacle of David in Mt. Zion, we learn that the priests in the Tabernacle of David did not offer animal sacrifices. Instead, the ministry of singers and musicians offered up sacrifices of praise and thanksgiving. The Tabernacle of David was also different in that it did not have an Outer Court, nor did it have any furniture except for the Ark of the Covenant. It also did not have a Holy Place. The priests could boldly enter the Holy of Holies. There was no veil between them and the Ark.

In Jeremiah 3:16, the prophet tells us the Ark would not be remembered or sought after. The truth is that the Ark has never been found since the destruction of the Temple by the King of Babylon during the days of the Prophet Jeremiah. When Ezra and Nehemiah restored the Temple, they did not have the Ark. For that reason, the shekinah glory was not present. Even though the Mosaic law was carried on when Jesus was on this earth, the Temple had no Ark and no glory because Jesus was the fulfillment of the law.

The Mosaic covenant continued for about 40 years after the crucifixion and resurrection of Christ. In A.D. 70, God allowed the material Temple to be destroyed. Those who accepted Jesus Christ as the promised Messiah became known as Christians.

Today, we should worship God, both individually and corporately, according to the Tabernacle of David if we desire to be in the center of God's will. Jeremiah 31:4 says, "Again I will build thee, and thou shalt be built, O virgin of Israel: thou shalt again be adorned with thy tabrets, and shalt go forth in the dances of them that make merry." And Jeremiah 31:12-13 states:

> *Therefore they shall come and sing in the height of Zion, and shall flow together to the goodness of the Lord, for wheat, and for wine, and for oil, and for the young of the flock and of the herd: and their soul shall be as a watered garden; and they shall not sorrow any more at all. Then*

shall the virgin rejoice in the dance, both young men and old together: for I will turn their mourning into joy, and will comfort them, and make them rejoice from their sorrow (Jeremiah 31:12-13).

When Judah was taken into bondage by the Babylonians, the dance was lost. In Lamentations 5:15, we see this take place: "The joy of our heart is ceased; our dance is turned into mourning."

When we are in spiritual bondage, we lose our joy and we have no desire to dance. The Church corporately has been in periods of bondage throughout the centuries. We are told in Scripture that where the Spirit of the Lord is, there is liberty. When we go to a football game, we jump, shout, cheer, and wave our hands in support of our team. When our team is losing, we shout even more to encourage the players and to show them our support. Why is our body unable to contain itself during this period of excitement? Is it because we are a spirit that has a soul and live in a body? Is it that our soul, the connection between our spirit and our body, desires to express what it is feeling?

I beseech you therefore, brethren, by the mercies of God, that ye present your bodies a living sacrifice, holy, acceptable unto God, which is your reasonable service (Romans 12:1).

What is holiness? According to the commentary in the King James Bible (Leviticus, KJV Open Bible Edition, Thomas Nelson Publishers, 1975, p. 95 paragraph 8 "Holiness"), holiness is defined as obedience. "The root meaning of the word holiness is separation, and every regulation of diet and worship was intended to preserve this difference from all other people." Likewise, the dance in the Church is different than the dance of the world. It is not sensual. It does not magnify the dancer. Rather, the dancer magnifies God, and the dance is an expression of praise to God.

This same commentary also defines sacrifice. "Originally, a sacrifice was simply a gift. A gift to God as an expression of love and gratitude. It reminded the worshiper that he must offer God the costly gift of life."

Let's see how the two definitions listed above apply to the dance. Let us first consider obedience. What has God called us to do in Psalm 149 and Psalm 150? He has told us to praise Him in the dance. Psalm 149:3 says, "Let them praise His name in the dance: Let them sing praises unto Him with the timbrel and harp." Where has He called us to do this? In verse 1 of Psalm 149 we are told to do it "in the congregation of saints." We are also called to do this at home as we minister unto Him.

Why has He called us to dance before Him? Psalm 149:7-9 says, "To execute vengeance upon the heathen, and punishments upon the people; to bind their kings with chains, and their nobles with fetters of iron; to execute upon them the judgment written: This honour have all His saints...."

Since we established that holiness is obedience, then are we going to obey? Ephesians 6:12 tells us, "For we wrestle not against flesh and blood, but against principalities, against powers, against the rulers of the darkness of this world, against spiritual wickedness in high places."

God's ways are higher than our ways. He takes the foolish things of this world to confound the wise. Who would think that God would use dance to put the enemy to flight? "And ye shall tread down the wicked; for they shall be ashes under the soles of your feet in the day that I shall do this, saith the Lord of hosts" (Mal. 4:3). God inhabits the praises of His people. As we form a habitation for Him through our praises, His anointing comes and destroys the yokes. Individually and corporately, we are the temple not made with human hands that God seeks to inhabit. Although God is always with us, the manifestation of His presence intensifies as He invites us to worship Him.

Now, let us consider sacrifice. We said sacrifice is a gift to God. Sometimes we don't feel like dancing. It is during those times that we probably need to praise God the most because we are probably under spiritual attack. It is at this time that dancing before the Lord becomes a sacrifice because we do not feel like dancing or singing.

I remember once I felt very sick and had no strength to move. I knew I was under heavy attack from the enemy. I forced myself to get out of bed. I put on some praise music and began to dance before the Lord. It was a hard thing to do. Little by little, I started feeling the presence of the spiritual force of joy entering my body. I started getting so excited about God that my praise turned into worship. As I worshiped God, the symptoms left and I experienced divine healing.

The devil knows the power in dance and that is why he has fought to keep the people of God in our generation ignorant in the matter. Praise the Lord; God is greater than satan and His truths shall go forth in the earth until the kingdoms of this world have become the kingdoms of our God and of His Son Jesus Christ. The Holy Spirit will teach us and guide us into all truth if we open our hearts to receive His truth—which always points us to Jesus Christ, the King of Kings and the God of Gods.

In our generation, we have seen waves of revival. Along with each wave, a truth that had been stolen from the Church has been restored. The only problem has been that each truth that has been restored to the Church has become an idol around which a denomination has been formed. As a result, the participants in that wave of the Holy Spirit have become like the Pharisees of Jesus' time. They received their portion of truth, but when the next wave of restoration came, they closed their mind to it and became an enemy of the new wave of the Holy Spirit. However, in each generation God has maintained a remnant who chose to move when the cloud (the present move of God, or the glory of God) moved. As for the ones who chose not to move with the cloud, "Ichabod" was written over their doorpost for "the glory has departed" (see 1 Sam. 4:21). They continue with a form of religion, but deny the power thereof (see 1 Tim. 3:5). These dead churches are what satan is using to persecute the Church.

As we get closer to the second coming of Christ, the darkness becomes darker while the light becomes brighter. It is time that we take our place in the army of God and stop fighting each other and start fighting the forces of darkness. We must stop competing with each other and start helping each other. For how can we say we love God whom we have not seen when we cannot love each other whom we do see? (See First John 4:20.)

Television was invented so that we could preach the gospel to all the world. Yet, because we have become so spiritually minded, we have become no earthly good. It is time we get angry and take back what Jesus paid the price for. Why should our children be subjected to violent shows on TV and other demonic influences? It is time we take back the arts for God. We can preach the gospel through drama, dance, music, movies, and other art forms. God is going to hold us accountable for what we have done with this earth during our generation. All it takes is one person with a dream like Joseph to change the world.

It took just one woman to get prayer out of the schools. Why do we sit back and let our schools go down the tubes when the resurrection power that raised Jesus from the dead abides in us? We want the power of God, but we don't want to pay the price of being rejected or talked about. It is time we get radical for Jesus! After all, we are His body in the earth. We are His hands to touch lives, His feet to go where life is needed. We are the salt of the earth. Have we lost our flavor? I pray not.

Now that we have a better understanding of the Tabernacles of Moses and David, let us look into the Temple of Solomon. The word *temple*, according to *Webster's II New Revised University Dictionary*, is defined as: "A place or building dedicated to the worship or the presence of a deity.... Something held to contain a divine presence." In contrast to the word *temple*, the word *tabernacle* is defined as: "The portable sanctuary in which the Jews carried the Ark of the Covenant through the desert...." Notice that a tabernacle is portable, whereas a temple is permanent! The Tabernacles of Moses and David were portable, whereas the Temple of Solomon was permanent.

The staves that were used to transport the Ark of the Covenant were removed when the Ark of the Covenant came into the Temple of Solomon, signifying that the journey of the Ark was finished. It found a resting place. Our heart is the Temple of Solomon. It is a building not made by human hands where the law has been written in the tablets of our heart.

Let us see how this relates to the Tabernacles of Moses and David. The Tabernacle of Moses in Mt. Gibeon represented God-ordained rules and regulations as well as God-ordained sacrificial offerings. It was a place of ceremonial washings where the priests ministered to God on behalf of *sacrifice of Praise.*

the nation of Israel. It was ritualistic. It was a place where the people could not go behind the veil.

On the other hand, the Tabernacle of David was a place where one could become intimate with God. There were no rituals, no sacrificing of animals, but only sacrifices of praise. It was a place of spontaneity where one could dance and sing and praise God. It was a place where the prophetic took place and the song of the Lord was heard.

The Temple of Solomon incorporated both the form and order of the Tabernacle of Moses with the spontaneity of the Tabernacle of David.

For the glory of God to be revealed, the fullness of the Godhead must be present. We must have the "way," which is God's plan; we must have the "truth," which is God's Word; and we must have the "life," which is Jesus manifested through the liberty of the Holy Spirit (see Jn. 14:6). We can say that God lives in our hearts if we have made a covenant with God by having Jesus be Lord of our life.

Religious traditions have deceived many by leading them to believe that going to church is enough. The devil goes to church and even believes in Jesus, but he does not obey Him. To believe in Jesus Christ means to change our way of living by living according to the Word of God as the Holy Spirit directs us. Knowing the Scripture is essential. How can we hear the voice of God if we don't know His Word? We must know the Jesus of the Bible and not the Jesus of the New Age.

The Temple of Solomon foreshadows the heavenly Jerusalem, which is mentioned in the Book of Revelation. It is the completed Temple of God where His glory dwells. It is the finished Temple, not made by human hands, where there are no more tears, no more sickness, and no more sorrow. "And I heard a great voice out of heaven saying, Behold, the tabernacle of God is with men, and He will dwell with them, and they shall be His people, and God Himself shall be with them, and be their God" (Rev. 21:3).

In summary, the Temple of Solomon was a place where the order of the Tabernacle of Moses was followed, and the liberty and spontaneity of the Tabernacle of David was incorporated to provide a place of ruling and reigning, authority, dominion, and liberty.

Jesus puts the law in our hearts as we come to Him by faith. The Holy Spirit puts liberty in our being. "Where the Spirit of the Lord is, there is liberty" (2 Cor. 3:17). All authority and dominion was given unto Jesus, as a result of His blood being shed for us on Calvary, and Jesus passed it on to us, His Body. He said we would be able to do greater things than He did because He went to sit at the right hand of the Father.

As Solomon followed the order and pattern that was given to David by God in First Chronicles 28:11-21 and 25:1-8 in the construction of the Temple and in the order of worship, so must we follow it today if we want the glory of God to fall on our congregation.

Order of worship

TABERNACLE OF MOSES	TABERNACLE OF DAVID	T O
Synonymous with:	Synonymous with:	Sy
Mt. Sinai	Mt. Zion	Mt.
Mt. Gibeon	Grace	Fina
The Law	No Outer Court	Permanence
Wilderness	No Holy Place	Staves Removed
Aaronic Priesthood	No Veil	Temple of God
Incense as Worship	No Animal Sacrifice after the Dedication	Body of Christ
Animal Sacrifices	Continuous Sacrifice of Praise	Kingdom Order
Glory Only in Most Holy Place	Intimacy With God	Continuous Praise and Worship
Only High Priest Could Enter the Most Holy Place	Great Number of Singers Dancers (Chorus), Musicians	The City of God
Abiather	Zadok	The Bride of Christ Law in Man's Heart

(Note: David allowed the Tabernacle of Moses to remain under Abiather the Priest, while the Tabernacle of David was in use and held the Ark. Since there was no Ark in the Tabernacle of Moses, there was no glory in it. Some churches today are dead because they, like the Pharisees of Jesus' time, live by the law and not by faith in the finished work of Jesus Christ.)

Choros

(Greek)

Denotes and enclosure for dancing;
hence a company of dancers and singers.

Choreography

(Greek-Khoreia)

A choral dance, the art of creating
and arranging dances or ballets.

Chapter 4

Types and Purposes of Dance in the Church

In this chapter we will look at the various types of dance in the church. These are the praise dance, worship dance, warfare dance, celebration dance, travail dance, prophetic dance, and dances for special occasions including ordinations, weddings, funerals, baby dedications, and evangelism. When I first started dancing in the church, I did not have an understanding of the whole picture concerning dance. I started out in obedience to the anointing of the Holy Spirit with fear and trembling. I was very concerned to not offer strange fire before the Lord (see Lev. 10:1; Num. 3:4). As I stepped out in faith, the Holy Spirit was my teacher and showed me how to move. I then started studying to show myself approved of God. I started searching Scripture. I also went to the library and did research on the Jewish customs concerning dance. Little by little, the Holy Spirit unveiled to me what I believe is the pattern God would have us use in corporate gatherings. God is the God of order and is very specific about the patterns He gives us to follow.

In all that God does there is a rhyme and a reason. Nothing is an accident with God. Like people do in many churches today, I started dancing only when I felt the anointing. I thought that was the only time I was to dance. We called it "dancing in the Spirit." Later on, as I sought the Lord and studied the Scripture, I found out that was only one form of dance. Like the prophetic song of the Lord, this type of dance is a prophetic dance. Precept upon precept, the Lord Jesus Christ gave me insight into the many types of dance and the purpose for each one.

Praise Dance

The first dance we will study is the praise dance. As we studied in the previous chapters, praise is not based on how we feel or if we feel anything. Praise is based on covenant. God ordained us to praise Him. Throughout Scripture, we find the Word of the Lord admonishing us to praise. Here are some Scripture verses you may want to study concerning praise:

> *Praise ye the Lord. Praise the Lord, O my soul. While I live will I praise the Lord: I will sing praises unto my God while I have any being* (Psalm 146:1-2).

Here the person who wrote this psalm is speaking to his soul and telling it to praise God. Obviously, he was not in the mood for praising God so he had to speak to his mind and command it to praise God in the midst of whatever he was going through.

> *Praise ye the Lord. Sing unto the Lord a new song, and His praise in the congregation of saints. ... Let them praise His name in the dance: let them sing praises unto Him with the timbrel and harp* (Psalm 149:1,3).

> *Praise Him with the timbrel and dance: praise Him with stringed instruments and organs* (Psalm 150:4).

Praise then is something we do by faith because God has commanded us to do it. As in all God commands us to do, praise is for our own good. It is our way into the Holy of Holies. Praise invites the manifested presence of God since, as we are told in Scripture, God inhabits the praises of His people.

Perhaps we can gain greater insight into praise dance by observing what the pastor and the praise singers do in preparation for the midweek and Sunday services. The pastor prepares a sermon and studies the Scripture in preparation for delivering the message he feels God wants to give to the congregation. The singers have a practice during the week where they practice the songs they will sing during the service.

During the service, the singers and musicians start offering the sacrifice of praise by singing pre-rehearsed songs. As they sing the songs, the anointing falls on them and they start singing a song of the Lord that has never been sung in the earth before. The Holy Spirit takes over the song service and the song leader is no longer in charge. The wind of the Holy Spirit blows on the sails of the ship and gives it the direction He wants it to go in.

In like manner, the pastor starts out preaching a prepared message until the Holy Spirit takes over. How many times have you heard a pastor say, "I had planned to go one direction, but the Holy Spirit is leading me in a different direction."

So it is with the dance team. They practice by faith to learn how to move in rhythm and in order. They practice to learn movement vocabulary. They may practice the prepared songs with the singers and musicians and choreograph the movements for each song. But like the musicians and the pastor, when the wind of the Holy Spirit and Jesus Christ the Lord of the dance takes over, the dancers start, moving according to the leading of the Holy Spirit with steps that are spontaneously given to them of the Holy Ghost.

Just as a computer cannot print anything unless a program is placed in it, so the dancer cannot dance if there is no dance vocabulary in her or him. Once the dance vocabulary is placed in a person, the Holy Spirit will arrange and rearrange the steps He chooses. God has called us to be a people of excellence, so we must train those whom God has called to dance before Him so His beauty can be revealed through them. We can all sing corporately in church, but we do not allow a person who has no voice to do a solo. Similarly, in the dance we can all dance when the Holy Spirit calls for corporate dance, but we must have skillful dancers who can dance during the praise and worship service.

I believe the Holy Spirit has shown me that the dance team should dance during the praise part of the service. As the congregation is taken into worship, then God will anoint those He wants to move through. At that point, the dancers may continue to dance or the Holy Spirit may want them to sit down, depending on what and how God wants to move. He will then choose the vessels or vessel He wants to move through.

Thus, the praise dance is done by faith or it can be choreographed. This will prepare the way for the prophetic dance or prophetic song, spoken prophecy, healing, or any other manifestation of the Holy Spirit. It also prepares the hearts of the people to receive the preached Word of God. It is like wine that is taken with bread. Bread alone is dry and a person can choke on it. Praise is the wine that makes it easy to chew the bread of the Word.

The praise dance team should dance in unity, not with each individual doing his or her own movement. They should have a leader whom they should follow as they dance.

I was looking at a video that was taken du_
church services. I rejoiced at what the Holy S_
our dancing. It looked like the dance was cl_
but it was not. The dance team learned to foll_ _...als
taught to them, and thus we moved in unity, yet with creativity, to give the dance form. We incorporated change of levels, change of direction, variety of formations such as circles, lines, diagonals, and scattered formations. Our movements depicted what the words of the song were saying. It was difficult at first to find movements to correspond with the words sung. As the team matured in the dance, the Holy Spirit taught us how to express words through body movements. (In the segment of dance terminology in Chapter 7, we will look at ways in which to give dance form, meaning, and depth.)

To better understand praise, I have included the seven Hebrew words for praise:

Barak: This means to bless, to praise, to kneel, and to salute (Judg. 5:2).

Halal: This means to shine, to be clamorously foolish, to rave, to celebrate, and to boast (1 Chron. 16:4).

Shabach: This means to shout, to triumph, to command, and to glory (Lk. 19:37-39).

Tehillah: This means "war praise," high praise, and it involves God responding to our faith (Ps. 22:3).

Todah: This means to offer the sacrifice of praise, especially choir of worshipers, choreography, processions (Ps. 50:23).

Yadah: This means lifting hands and lifting heart publicly (2 Chron. 20:19-21).

Zamar: This means singing praise and playing instruments (Ps. 57:7; 1 Chron. 15:16).

In summary, the sacrifice of praise is the zealous freewill offering of our actions, our expressions, through the movement of dance as we present our bodies as living sacrifices unto the Lord, as we extol the character of God and His works through the dance. The movements can include clapping of hands, jumping, leaping, bowing, skipping, and any other movement the Holy Spirit inspires. These movements or expressions are offered by faith and have nothing to do with feelings. Praise dance is a covenantal response to God's command in Psalm 149 and 150 to praise Him in the dance in the midst of the congregation.

Worship Dance

The next dance we will look at is the worship dance. As mentioned earlier, worship is a privilege. We cannot worship God on our own. The Holy Spirit, as we praise God, brings us into worship. We cannot just turn worship on. Worship is God manifesting Himself to us and through us in response to our praise. Worship is initiated by God as we humble ourselves before Him. Worship is the key to experiencing the knowledge of God. It is during worship that God may choose to speak to us prophetically through the spoken word, through a prophetic dance, through a prophetic song, or through a prophetic drama.

As we receive the word of the Lord during worship, the anointing will heal us, encourage us, exhort us, direct us, correct us, or show us what the mind of God is for the hour. God will choose how He wants to express Himself during worship. We may experience a time of silence in which God reveals His holiness, or God may choose to have the dance team do a worship dance during which people get healed as the anointing flows through the dancers. He may choose to express Himself through the pastor in the laying on of hands or through a word of knowledge. He may choose to sing through someone to bring deliverance to one or more people. He may choose to take the congregation into a warfare mode for a country, a church, or an individual.

We have had the Lord manifest Himself as a warrior at one of our services as He led us to pray and do warfare for Africa. In this instance, the entire congregation entered in and did corporate warfare. The Holy Spirit instructed us to use banners and to march in a circle. He then instructed the men to do the warfare as the women clapped their hands to the beat of the music.

At a conference in Atlanta, Georgia, God chose to send a healing anointing for marriages by instructing all the husbands and wives to come to the front of the church and dance together as the musicians played the song of the Lord, a spontaneous song given to the musicians by the Holy Spirit—a prophetic song.

When the worship anointing lifts, we will experience different reactions based on how God chose to express Himself to us. If He expressed His holiness, we may experience a time of silence. If He expressed His healing power, we will be filled with joy and thanksgiving. In this case, we will praise Him for what He has done. If this attitude of thanksgiving continues for a prolonged time, we may enter into worship again and thus go into a second circle of praise and worship.

In our church, we have experienced several circles, which lasted for hours. We started service at 10:00 a.m. and did not get out of church until 3:00 p.m. Who wants to go home when you can be in the presence of the anointing of God?

Unfortunately, not many churches are willing to let God be God in a service. They have their own agenda that God has to follow instead of the church following God's agenda. Consequently, people miss out on experiencing the anointing of God to the fullest.

After the circle of praise and worship is concluded, the preaching of the Word of God will follow. Sometimes the preaching will be done through what took place during worship and the pastor will not have to preach that day. Let God be God and do as He pleases. His ways are higher than ours and more effective!

In summary, the worship dance comes after we as living sacrifices have been consumed spirit, soul, and body at the altar of praise. The fire of God burns all the chaff that we came to church burdened down with. Worry, sin-consciousness, doubt, unbelief, and unforgiveness are done away with as we meditate on the attributes of God and as we sing and dance as a reminder of our covenant with God and of His promises to us. Faith rises up and we remember how great God is. As we decrease and He increases, the Holy Spirit inhabits our praises and invites us to worship.

Worship movements will be choreographed by the Holy Spirit. Usually the music will be slow and the movements will be soft, flowing, ballet-type movements. They will be movements where we bow down and adore our King or movements of love and adoration to our Bridegroom. Worship is the connection of our spirit to God's Spirit, bypassing the soulish realm. It is the time God will speak to us. As we worship God, He may choose to lead us into a warfare mode, a prophetic word, or a healing anointing. If during worship God chooses to lead us into warfare, the dance movements will be sharp and warlike and the music will also be sharp and warlike. If He expresses Himself as the God of joy, the dance steps will be joyful steps as will the music be joyful.

Warfare Dance

The warfare dance is the next dance we will study.

> *Let them praise His name in the dance: let them sing praises unto Him with the timbrel and harp. ... To execute vengeance*

vengence

upon the heathen, and punishments upon the people; to bind their kings with chains, and their nobles with fetters of iron (Psalm 149:3,7-8).

*For by thee I have **run** through a troop; and by my God have I **leaped** over a wall. ... He maketh my feet like hinds' feet, and setteth me upon my high places. He teacheth my hands to war, so that a bow of steel is broken by mine arms. ... I have pursued mine enemies, and overtaken them: neither did I turn again till they were consumed. ... Great deliverance giveth He to His king; and sheweth mercy to His anointed, to David, and to his seed for evermore* (Psalm 18:29,33-34,37,50).

And the God of peace shall bruise Satan under your feet shortly. The grace of our Lord Jesus Christ be with you. Amen (Romans 16:20). *Lilian*

Neither yield ye your members as instruments of unrighteousness unto sin: but yield yourselves unto God, as those that are alive from the dead, and your members as instruments of righteousness unto God (Romans 6:13). *Lilian*

God takes the things that are foolishness to the world to confound the wise (see 1 Cor. 1:27). He had Joshua *march* around Jericho for seven days. On the seventh day the wall fell down as they marched around and shouted for the seventh time. God had Naaman dip in the river seven times before he was healed. Who are we to challenge the God of the universe on how to fight the battle?

Lucifer's fall was brought about because he wanted to be exalted above God. Since he was the cherub who was the praise and worship leader in the heavenlies, he hates when *enemy* God's people praise the Lord. He does warfare against God through song and dance. We can see an example of this in today's rock music. Most of it has words that encourage suicide, drugs, sex outside of marriage, and rebellion against

satan

authority. This music stirs the lust of the flesh and is expressed in seductive dances and dances that cause teenagers to go into a frenzy. (The word *frenzy* in *The Reader's Digest Family Word Finder* [Pleasantville, New York: The Reader's Digest Association, Inc., 1977, p. 328] is defined as: "1. Fit, seizure, outburst, furor, delirium, madness, fury, distraction, hysteria, obsession, craze, mania. 2. Mental agitation, turmoil, state: mad rush, great haste.")

It is no wonder that satan has opposed the dance in the Church. He knows the power it has (see Psalm 149) to destroy his works of darkness.

Another good example of satan copying God's ways and perverting them is when people get drunk from alcohol. We are told in the New Testament to be drunk with the Spirit and not with wine. What does the devil do? He gets people into bondage to alcoholism, which brings destruction to families, communities, and society as a whole.

What is God's alternative to alcoholism? To be filled with the Holy Spirit. What do we experience when we are filled with the Holy Spirit? We experience the euphoria that the alcoholic is looking for, but it does not cost money. It is a free gift from God. We don't have a hangover after the effects wear out, and we don't risk getting into a car accident or a fight. How do we get this euphoria? By praising God. He inhabits the praises of His people. The less there is of us, the more there is of Him. Sometimes God may choose to manifest His presence to us even when we are not praising Him. It comes to us at His choosing or we can choose to enter in by praising Him.

When a need is made known, the dance of warfare can be done by faith to bring deliverance to a city, country, congregation, family, or individual. It can be choreographed or spontaneous.

46

During one of our services on Sunday, we were interceding for men to come into our church, since most of the congregation consisted of women. The Lord, through our praise and worship team, led us to get the men who were present at that service to get up, dance, and do warfare for men who were not in the church so that they would be released from bondage and come to salvation and into the house of God. Women were instructed to sit down and pray in the Spirit while the men danced with banners and did warfare. Our church is now filled with men.

The dance of warfare, as well as the praise dance, is used to prepare the atmosphere for the preaching of the Word.

As the praise and worship dance team leader, there were times when I would come into the church and feel oppressive spirits lurking around the sanctuary. It was difficult to dance, but as we offered the sacrifice of praise or did a warfare dance, one could feel the oppression lift. Now the people were ready to receive the preaching of the Word.

It is good to remember that when a church is first started, one has to dethrone the prince of the power of the air that has been on assignment to that location. The struggles a new church will have in getting started will depend on how deeply entrenched the powers of darkness are in a location. The more intercession, praise and worship, warfare, and binding and loosing that goes on, the quicker the church will experience victory. One can really feel the liberty in the service as the forces of darkness are destroyed. It takes less praise to enter into worship once the land has been possessed. As the church grows, however, people who cause strife and division may come in and you have to go back to warfare and lengthy praise to get into the anointing.

With the same principle, the warfare dance can be used at home to win territory for your loved ones, community, business, school system, and government in your community, or to intercede for the nation.

My husband and I were separated for 15 months and the Lord had me dance at home to do warfare on his behalf. Sometimes dancing was the last thing on earth I wanted to do, but that is when I knew I needed to do it the most because I could feel the oppression around our family. Now my husband is back, and most people cannot get over how much he has changed. He is a greater father and husband. It has been a wonderful testimony to my neighbors who watched my unconditional love and forgiveness and faith in God. As a result of this victory, many of my neighbors have gotten saved. In their time of trouble, they came to me because they saw that my God was real and that He answered prayer. As I prayed for my husband God also changed me and is still molding and shaping me into His image.

Most of the time, the movements used in a warfare dance are sharp and angular. Examples would be kicks, jumps, punches, lunging, falling, stabbing, pushing, leaping, turning, clapping, stomping, marching, and pulling. As you seek the Lord in choreographing a dance, He will give you the steps. When it is a spontaneous dance, the Holy Spirit will dance through you and will create the steps as you go along. You do, however, have to have a dance vocabulary in you just as you must have the Word of God in you in order for the Holy Spirit to bring it to your remembrance. Of course, we cannot put God in a box. If He could make a donkey talk, He can make a lame man dance. However, we must keep in mind that the donkey talking was an exception to the rule. So, liturgical dancers should prepare themselves to the best of their ability so that as they dance in the liberty of the Holy Spirit, the glory and beauty of God can be revealed through them.

Warfare dance can be used to bring deliverance, healing, financial breakthrough, ministry breakthrough, and anything else that is needed. I use this dance a lot to get break-throughs for my family. I start by playing music tapes with words that pertain to my situation. I dance in my kitchen. (That is my altar of prayer where I meet God.) I start out by faith. When the anointing falls, the Holy Spirit gives me songs and words to sing. At that point, I shut the tape recorder off. I dance to the words and songs that the Holy Spirit brings to my mind. I address the powers, principalities, and rulers of darkness as the Holy Spirit gives me their names. I bind them and command them to cease their operation. I command them to leave the person, business, or ministry that I am warring for. As I am verbally singing or speaking, the Holy Spirit gives me corresponding hand and feet movements.

When the war has been won in the heavenlies I know it by the joy that comes or by the liberty that comes. Sometimes it takes a few seconds. Sometimes it takes a few days. Sometimes it takes months. This is not to say one dances without stopping. Rather, one dances until the Holy Spirit unction leaves. When it is a long battle, the Holy Spirit will lead you on a daily basis as to what is needed each day. It is a lot less burdensome to battle through dance than to battle through dry prayers. It works every time. This can be done corporately or individually at home. Through warfare dance we can know that our prayers will be answered.

In summary, the warfare dance is an aggressive dance filled with sharp movements and sounds such as kicks, stabbing motions, falling, struggle-type moves, punches, feet stomping, death blows, righteous indignation, loud cymbals, drums, marching, yelling, and praying out loud in tongues or in English. It can include marching around the sanctuary, around the block, or around a community. It can include the carrying of flags and banners. It could be a Jerico march like Joshua did to put the devil to flight. It can start out with the praise and worship dance team and end up with the whole congregation involved. It can start out with anger at what the devil has stolen from us and end up with shouts of victory as we sense a breakthrough in the spirit realm.

Psalm 18:38-39,42 says, "I have wounded them that they were not able to rise: they are fallen under my feet. For Thou hast girded me with strength unto the battle ["The joy of the Lord is your strength" (Neh. 8:10)]: Thou subdued under me those that rose up against me. … Then did I beat them small as the dust before the wind: I did cast them out as the dirt in the streets." This was the prophetic song by King David who was a dancer before the Lord.

Dance of Celebration

Another form of dance is the dance of celebration.

The Reader's Digest Family Word Finder defines the word celebrate as follows: "1. commemorate, observe; engage in festivities, ceremonialize. 2. Proclaim, broadcast, acclaim, praise, extol, venerate, honor, exalt, applaud, laud, cheer, commend, revere. 3. Observe, solemnize, hallow, consecrate, honor, ritualize, bless, glorify."

Thus, another name for the dance of celebration is a festive dance. We can dance to celebrate the birth of Jesus Christ. We can dance to celebrate the resurrection of Jesus Christ. We can dance to celebrate our soon coming Bridegroom. We can dance to celebrate a personal victory or a corporate or family victory.

In the Old Testament, the Israelites were commanded by God to appear before the Lord in the sanctuary three times a year. They were commanded to celebrate Passover in Deuteronomy 16:1. They were commanded to celebrate the Feast of Harvest, which in the New Testament is known as the Day of Pentecost when the Holy Spirit fell on the disciples in the upper room in Acts 2:1-4. (The Feast of Harvest is found in Exodus 23:16.) The third festival was the Feast of Tabernacles mentioned in Deuteronomy 16:13-15. This was a feast to celebrate the harvest. Today it is significant that God, through the Holy Spirit, tabernacles in us, and God is gathering in the last great harvest of souls before the second coming of Christ.

Now let us look at the three festivals in the New Testament accounts while Jesus was on the earth. First, we have the Feast of Passover in the Gospel of Matthew. In it we see Jesus cleansing the Temple and saying, "My house shall be called the house of prayer." As dancers, we must keep our "temple" from being defiled by the contamination of this world. We must be people of prayer.

We find that the Feast of Passover is associated with healing. Exodus 12 and Psalm 105:37 tell us that Israel was healed as they fed upon the body of the Passover lamb. Thus, as we celebrate the Lord in festival dances, healing will take place as the Holy Spirit pours out God's anointing. For this reason, dancers must have pure motives. They must be prayed up and filled with the Holy Ghost so they can be used as channels of God to bring healing to the congregation.

Passover is also associated with the body and blood of Jesus Christ. Jesus did the miracle of the feeding of the multitude and taught His disciples that He was the bread of life during the Feast of Passover. Thus, we can celebrate holy communion with a festival dance to remind the congregation of the power of the blood and body of Jesus. Jesus ministered at the feasts and at the Passover festival and taught that He is the atonement for all sin. Thus, we can celebrate that we are forgiven by faith and not by works.

The second festival is the Feast of Tabernacles, which was marked by peculiar rites, sacrifices, joyous festivities, and dwelling in booths. Here in the New Testament account we see Jesus' triumphant entry into Jerusalem with the people waving palm branches as He passed by them. This feast also included a ceremony of the drawing out of waters, which was not included in the Mosaic law. This spoke of the Holy Spirit who would be poured out when Jesus was glorified. As we dance before the Lord, He inhabits the praises of His people and pours out in the midst of the congregation His manifested presence. Thus, as we either corporately or individually dance before the Lord, He will pour out a visitation that will bring enlightenment to us concerning His doctrine and His Word or bring direction to our lives.

Thus we see that Jesus is both the water and the light. As we dance before the Lord, we need to make our prayer that anyone who is in darkness would come to the light as Jesus, the Lord of the dance (David is symbolic of Jesus, and he danced before the Lord), expresses Himself through the dancers.

The dances that were associated with this festival are the torch dance, processions of marching and singing people, and children carrying flags and candles. The flags are of the tribe of Judah, which means praise. Dances should be colorful and expressive.

Last, we see Jesus sending His Spirit on the Day of Pentecost, which was the third festival. Pentecost not only symbolizes the outpouring of the Holy Spirit, but also the uniting of the Jews and Gentiles into one body. "I will pour out of my Spirit upon *all* flesh..."(Acts 2:17). (Another example of this is found in the Old Testament in the story of Ruth, a Moabite, and Boaz, a Jew.) The procession and the circle dance were the main dances of the feast. Debbie Roberts, in her book, *Rejoice*, supports these ideas using this Scripture in Deuteronomy 16:9-11:

> *Seven weeks after the harvest begins, there shall be another festival before the Lord your God.... At that time bring to Him a free-will offering proportionate in size to His blessing*

upon you as judged by the amount of your harvest. It is a time to rejoice before the Lord with your family and household. And don't forget to include the local Levites, foreigners, widows, and orphans. Invite them to accompany you to the celebration at the sanctuary (Deuteronomy 16:9-11 TLB).

During this feast, the people rejoiced as they thanked God for the plentiful harvest and they offered it unto the Lord. As they marched to the appointed place of gathering, the people rejoiced as they marched to the music. Women and children danced and played joyfully as they praised God. The young girls wore flower garlands in their hair.

Thus, through studying how the Jewish people celebrated during the various feasts, we can see that a dance of celebration is a dance that can be done solo, in a group, in a circle, in a spontaneous fashion, or in a choreographed form. The movements will usually express joy, honor, exaltation, cheer, and reverence. Sample movements would be leaping, skipping, jumping, twirling, walking, hand clapping, and the like. Tambourines would be appropriate in a dance of celebration.

The dance of celebration is festive, colorful, and joyous. Props that can be used, depending on the occasion, include palm branches, flowers, candles, torches, streamers, and other ornamental items. Costumes can be colorful, or they may be white if depicting the Holy Spirit.

Dance of Travail

The next dance we will study is the dance of travail. The dance of travail is a dance of faith where we thank God for the answer to our prayer before the answer is visible. In this dance, we proclaim to the principalities of darkness that our God is able to do above and beyond what we ask of Him. It is similar to a war dance. Dancing the dance of travail gives he things God desires to establish in the earth to fulfill His purposes.

One can travail through prayer by speaking the Word and praying in the Spirit. I have found, however, that travailing in the dance is more joyful and less wearisome. There is a greater release that takes place when we travail in the dance. First of all, the adrenaline that is released in our body when we are angry, worried, or fearful dissipates as we move our body and use up energy through movement. Second, something happens in the spirit realm when we move. "Let them praise His name in the dance...to bind their kings with chains, and their nobles with iron" (Ps. 149:3,8).

I make up my own songs, inspired by the Holy Spirit and the Word of God. The Holy Spirit gives me the tunes as I step out in faith and start singing. I may start out sounding out of tune, but by the time the Holy Spirit gets through travailing through me, I am filled with the joy of the Lord and have a *rhema* word engraved in my heart concerning my situation. The Holy Spirit can do this at home or during a church service. The movements can be warfare movements, movements of supplication, movements expressing power and authority, or a combination of several things. (By the way, a *rhema* word is a specific word received from God for a specific situation. It releases faith.)

As I mentioned in the segment on the warfare dance, dancing prepares the way for the Word to be preached. In other words, dancers, singers, and musicians war against the principalities of darkness that are on assignment to pastors, leaders, and people who are coming to the service so that everyone's ears will be ready to receive the preaching of the Word. They war against hindrances to the preacher so he or she may have the liberty of the Holy Ghost and the anointing to destroy the yokes of bondage people may have come in with.

Skillful musicians will pull on the heartstrings of the dancers, enabling the dancers to break into a higher realm in the Spirit. The dancers can only go as high as the musicians take them through their anointed music. If the musicians are off, it will cause the dancers to be off. It is important that dancers not be moved by their feelings. Dancers, as well as the musicians, must guard their emotions. It is important for a dancer to discern spirits so as not to allow the devil to use them to bring oppression into the camp.

When I first started dancing, the Holy Spirit enabled me to learn a lot of things firsthand. I'll never forget the first out-of-town conference I was invited to dance in. During the praise service, I felt the a tremendous oppression in the room. Since I was new in the dance of the church, I had a lot to learn. I thought that I was in sin or that God was displeased with me. I stopped in the middle of dancing and knelt in the middle of the sanctuary for fear God would strike me with fire from Heaven because of offering a sacrifice unacceptable to Him. The people in the congregation followed what I did, thinking that I was worshiping God.

Thank God for the prophet! One of the speakers at the conference was operating in the fivefold ministry as a prophet.

And he gave some, apostles; and some, prophets; and some, evangelists; and some, pastors and teachers; for the perfecting of the saints, for the work of ministry, for the edifying of the body of Christ (Ephesians 4:11).

The prophet brought correction and clarity to what was happening. First, he told the people to get up because they were not being honest with God. They were kneeling down because they saw me do it, not because they were paying homage to God. Then, he told the musician that he had yielded to a spirit of discouragement when he saw there were not as many people in the congregation as anticipated. The oppressive spirit that the musician had opened himself up to then tried to come upon the dancer (me) and then upon the congregation. It took us about 45 minutes to get from the outer court into the holy of holies because we had to do warfare to clear the heavenly atmosphere from the oppressive spirits.

Since musicians, singers, and dancers go ahead of the army, they are the first who are attacked. We need to discern the spirits around us. As musicians, singers, and dancers, we need to discern the spirits so as not to lead the congregation into bondage. It was during that experience that I learned not to yield to oppressive spirits and to discern the spirits that are not of God.

Another experience I had, which may help those of you who are as new in the dance as I was, had to do with a member of the dance team. Since it took me one to two hours (depending on the traffic) to get to the church the Lord sent me to, I had time to praise and worship the Lord while in my car. By the time I got to church, I was full of the joy of the Lord and of His anointing. I couldn't understand at first why every time we would get into a circle to pray as a dance team, I would sense oppression in the room. After a couple of weeks, I realized that the oppression we were fighting was not in the sanctuary per se, but it was coming from one of the other team members who had yielded to ill feelings against me. Thank God all is well now. That was one more experience the Lord allowed me to go through in order to write this book. Remember, the devil is the accuser of the brethren.

This experience taught me as a leader how to become a mother and love my spiritual children unconditionally. It taught me how to change spiritual diapers, clean up baby vomit, and nurture the babies to grow up to be mighty warriors for God—vessels of gold for the Master's use. It taught

me that iron sharpens iron and that God
one better watch what one prays for. This
by God to answer my prayer, "God, whate
me like Jesus. Make me a vessel of gold
Prune me. Shape me into Your Son's in
tremely painful, but the fruit this prayer yielded in my life
has been worth it. It has taught me to endure severe pressure, to love unconditionally, to forgive, to humble myself, to lay down my life so someone else may live. It has taught me discipleship. It sandpapered the areas in my life that were not pleasing to God. It helped me become more compassionate and more sensitive to the needs of others. It taught me not only how to be under authority, but also how to be in authority.

If you are going to be used of God to prepare the sanctuary for the Word to be preached, you cannot yield to jealousy, competition, gossip, hurt feelings, or any of the other lusts of the flesh, lusts of the eyes, or the pride of life. It is no longer you that lives, but Christ who lives in you (see Gal. 2:20). It will cost you a heavy price to be a vessel truly used of God.

In preparing the way for the Word of God to be preached, one must not yield to the spirits of darkness that may be lurking around the sanctuary, around your family, or around you. Discern what they are, resist them, take authority over them, and command them to depart. Then, set your face as a flint towards God, bring your emotions under the control of the Holy Spirit in you, and war them away as you dance. The battle is in the mind and we must bring into captivity every thought under the obedience of Christ.

As mentioned before in another section, you may not have to do much warring for the Word to go forth if the land has already been possessed and the giants who were on assignment to the area have been defeated. Your dance in that

...se will be a dance of celebration filled with liberty because God has given rest to your land.

In summary, the dance of travail is similar to the warfare dance. However, the dance of travail is a victory dance by faith. It is a confession or testimony before the manifestation is evident. It is a prevailing prayer as in Jacob wrestling with the angel until he, Jacob, prevailed. It is not agonizing that brings the promises, but it is believing that God is and that He is a rewarder of those who diligently seek Him. A dance of travail is a higher law of faith that moves God's hand.

In Hebrew, the word *chul-chul* means to whirl in a circular motion, to twist, to dance. It means to travail, to bring forth children, to writhe in pain. So go forth in the dance of travail and birth forth your personal *rhema* word from God. In a corporate church the dance team can travail to give birth to a prophecy or a *rhema* word for the church or for the pastor, elders, or person in the congregation. God wants to bring forth His promises into manifestation.

The movements of the dance of travail can vary according to the leading of the Holy Spirit. Usually they are circular, crouching as in giving birth, or as described above in the definition of *chul-chul*.

> *...for as soon as Zion travailed, she brought forth her children. Shall I bring to the birth, and not cause to bring forth? saith the Lord.... Rejoice ye with Jerusalem, and be glad with her, all ye that love her: Rejoice for joy with her, all ye that mourn for her: That ye may suck, and be satisfied with the breasts of her consolations; that ye may milk out, and be delighted with the abundance of her glory* (Isaiah 66:8-11).

Prophetic Dance

Another type of dance is the prophetic dance. The prophetic dance is a spontaneous dance that is inspired by the

Holy Spirit and danced by a single person or by a group of people. It is a dance where the mind of God is expressed so that the congregation not only hears the message from God, but also sees the message. An example of this type of dance in the Old Testament is found in First Samuel 18. After David had killed Goliath, the women of Israel came out singing and dancing. In their song, they proclaimed that David had killed 10,000 men when at that point he had only killed a lion, a bear, and Goliath.

The prophetic dance can be danced to a song of the Lord that is also spontaneous. It could be sung by the dancer or group of dancers. It could be sung by the pastor or the musicians. It could be sung by someone in the congregation or by the entire congregation. We have had experiences in our church where the pastor got a song of the Lord in which the congregation chanted back in answer to God, and we have had a prophetic dance where, as the leader of the dance team, I was led of the Holy Spirit to get the entire congregation to come out of their seats and to dance prophetically in response to God's Word.

God is an exciting, multi-faceted God. We cannot put Him in a box. He moves as He chooses. When the Holy Spirit has liberty to move in His church, the congregation will know they have had a manifestation of God in their midst.

The prophetic dance does not have to be danced to singing or instrumental music. It could be done to the rhythm of clapping hands, stomping feet, snapping fingers, or it can be done in silence. the prophetic dance can be a dance of warfare, a dance of edification, a dance of instruction, or a dance foretelling the world of events that are about to take place.

To move in the prophetic dance in an orderly fashion, it is helpful for the person or persons involved in the dance to know and understand prophecy. If a person does not normally move in the prophetic realm outside of the dance ministry, he or she will not properly be able to dance and prophesy at the same time. When the Holy Spirit calls us to do something, He equips us to do it. That is why we are instructed to "study to show ourselves approved." God does not want "cornflake" Christians representing Him and bringing dishonor to His name. That does not mean that we cannot make mistakes. Peter made mistakes at times and yet God still said to him, "Feed my sheep." We need to understand that in all we do for and through God, we must have a servant's heart and a teachable spirit. We will be called wise, as in Proverbs, if we have a teachable spirit. We will be fools if we do not allow those over us to bring the necessary correction to our lives.

The prophetic dance will be most effective when the musicians, the worship leader, the dance leader, and the pastor learn to flow together. When I first started leading the dance team in our church, I always would signal my pastor for approval or he would signal me for a confirmation that the Lord was calling for a prophetic dance. It took a lot of faith and courage for me to first step out into the prophetic realm.

Once, a visiting bishop came to our church. When he first saw me dancing he said to himself, "Flesh, flesh, flesh!" Instantly the Lord corrected him and he got up and shared with the congregation what had just gone on in his mind and how the Lord had corrected him. He then went on to prophesy to me. He said the Lord had told him how hard it was for me to get up and dance. He said the Lord told him, "The devil torments her after she is obedient and tells her that it was not God." He went on to say, "My daughter, the Lord wants you to know that from this day on, you will be known as the 'mother' of the dance. You are no longer to let the devil torment you. God wants you to know that He has called you to dance before Him. He knows the pain, rejection, and suffering you have been through. He will reward you for your obedience." (This took place in 1985.)

Pioneers experience many rejections, false accusations, and lonely hours that come as a result of their obedience to God. However, our reward is from the Lord. Jesus said that if they rejected Him, they will reject us. He also said we will learn obedience through suffering. As we suffer with Christ, so shall we rule and reign with Him.

I praise God that in all my trials He has given me the grace to forgive those who have accused me falsely. Through all this He has molded my character so that I am more able to love unconditionally. Because I humble myself before my accusers, God vindicates me and shows my innocence. Even today, people from my past have come to me after many years and asked my forgiveness for what they had done to me. Love never fails!

We must remember that we are not fighting against flesh and blood, but against powers, principalities, rulers of darkness, and wicked spirits in high places (see Eph. 6:12). We must also remember that the devil is the accuser of the brethren. We will beat the devil at his game if we respond in love and forgiveness toward our accusers. We must pray for them, for they know not what they do.

It is important for the dance leader to have the trust of her or his pastor. It enables her or him to flow freely. Trust is something that is developed by being around a person. A leader must be mentored by the pastor. In our church, the leadership stays after the service is over. We spend much time with our pastor learning from him. Like Jesus spent time with the disciples and shared things He would not share with the crowd, so we should spend time knowing our pastor and developing a close walk with him. This way he gets to know our strengths and our weaknesses. We need to let him correct us when we are wrong without being offended. A wise person will have a teachable spirit. It is also important that the dance leader be faithful and cooperative with the pastor. He is the head of the church on this earth and orders always come from the top down and not from the bottom up. A loving relationship and an attitude of cooperation must exist among the musicians, singers, dancers, and leadership of the house. It will hinder the flow of the Holy Spirit if there is strife among the members.

We have had occasions when there was disagreement between the members of one of the praise and worship departments and it was as evident as day. The musicians could not get it together; the dancers could not flow. It was like pulling teeth. Let's remember that we are building God's Kingdom and not our kingdom. We are just vessels to be filled by God to accomplish His purpose on this earth. Don't break ranks. Don't be like the prodigal son who wanted his inheritance ahead of his time. Wait for God's timing.

For us, all the years of trial and error have paid off. Our church moves beautifully in the praise and worship ministry. We all flow together and the Holy Spirit moves with liberty.

If you are just starting a dance team, I suggest you get together with the musicians so that you can practice and feel free to make mistakes in private. As you practice together and enter into the overflow of the anointing, you can feel free to do a prophetic dance. If there is any correction you need to receive, it can be done in private and you will not be embarrassed.

In the Old Testament, Elisha and Samuel had a school of the prophets (see 1 Sam. 19:18-24). They were trained how to operate in the prophetic. In our church, we have conferences in which the pastor allows us to practice, and brings direction, correction, instruction, and whatever else is necessary. It is a great help because it is done with a small group of people (about 20 people in a group). Somehow it is not as embarrassing to be corrected in front of 20 people as it is to be corrected in front of the whole congregation. By the way, if a prophecy is not from God, our pastor deals with it right away. He is not cruel or insensitive. He does it in love and it brings edification to the person in error. He usually will say, "We receive your word, Lord" after every prophetic utterance. If he does not say anything it means he did not believe it was God speaking prophetically.

There is much to say about the prophetic, but that is a whole other topic in itself. If you are interested in learning more about it, purchase a book on the prophetic ministry and do a study of the Bible concerning the prophetic. The attitude in which you go about it is important. If you go in looking to prove that it is not for today, your mind will be closed to the Holy Spirit. You will be like an old wineskin that will break when new wine is poured into it because it has become brittle with age and not able to take in the new. However, if you approach it with an open mind, there is no telling how much wine (illumination of the Scriptures) the Lord will pour out to you to fill up your new wine bottle.

Today, some people have problems believing in the existence of schools of prophets. I believe the reason is a lack of understanding. A school of the prophets does not make a person a prophet. Only God can do that. A school of the prophets is for anyone in the Body of Christ who wants better understanding concerning the prophetic. It is also for prophets to learn how to hear from God and how to be more effective in delivering the prophetic word. Just like pastors go to school to learn how to deliver God's Word and musicians go to school to become excellent, so prophets need grooming to become excellent in what they do. Jesus trained the disciples and the disciples trained the Timothys of their time. Let's stop killing our prophets. They are part of the Body of Christ. If one suffers, we all suffer.

There is no new revelation, for Scripture cannot be changed. However, there is illumination into God's Word that we need to understand as the Holy Spirit teaches us. Remember First Corinthians 14:3 tells us the purpose of prophecy is for edification, exhortation, and comfort. This applies to the prophetic dance also.

The Lord opened a door for my pastor to prophesy at the United Nations during a meeting commemorating a U.N. delegate who had passed away. Our dance team was invited to dance and the Lord allowed me to prophesy in dance and in word to the U.N. delegates. The prophecy was, "It is time for every nation to acknowledge you are God's creation." The dance our team danced was "We Shall Behold Him." The dance ended with one of the dancers running in holding small flags of all the countries and representing Jesus as He comes back to take dominion over the earth.

A person who is lacking in dance vocabulary tends to be more insecure and that hinders the anointing. However, don't let this discourage you if you are just starting to dance. Press on. Learn all you can. Do your best and God will do the rest. Remember, we all had to start somewhere. Keep your eyes on Jesus and He will move through you by the power of the Holy Spirit.

In summary, the prophetic dance should follow all the rules of prophecy. The only difference between the spoken prophecy and prophetic dance is that one is a verbal communication whereas the other is speaking through body language. One can verbally prophesy and at the same time interpret the prophecy through dance movement, thus unveiling God Himself through movement. Jesus said, "...he that hath seen Me hath seen the Father..." (Jn. 14:9). When we dance prophetically, it is the Spirit of God moving through us giving form to the spoken word. "...And the Spirit of God moved upon the face of the waters. And God said, Let there be light: and there was light" (Gen. 1:2-3).

Again, the prophetic dance will come after the sacrifice of praise has been consumed and when God then invites us into worship. It is during the worship time that God may choose to speak prophetically and/or dance prophetically through the worship team, a single dancer, or through an entire congregation. The movements can be any and all types depending on what God wants to speak. The prophecy may be done entirely through dance movements, without words. It can be done through words and dance. It can be done through instruments alone, without words or dance, or through instruments and dance and no words.

First Samuel 10:5-6 says: "...thou shalt meet a company of prophets coming down from the high place with a psaltery, and a tabret, and a pipe, and a harp, before them; and they shall prophesy." The prophets are released in a greater way by musical instruments that prophesy the song of the Lord. When Saul came upon the company of prophets, the spirit of prophecy came upon him and he prophesied. Thus, as we are united as living stones during our church services, the glory of God will fill the house, and we can all prophesy when the spirit of prophecy comes in the midst of us.

Ceremonial Dance

Besides dancing during church services and at home, the dance team can also dance during the following ceremonies or services:

1. Ordinations—Perhaps a processional may be in line before the service begins to show the solemnity and holiness of the occasion. It would also be appropriate to do a choreographed dance that would bring a

message to those being ordained or to the congregation on the seriousness of the occasion. The Lord may use a prophetic dance.

2. Wedding—There are many beautiful songs about the bride and groom that can be choreographed to show the covenant between a husband and wife. There can also be a round dance celebrating the union. The Lord may also release a prophetic dance.

3. Funeral—A dance to celebrate the union of the departed soul with God in Heaven may be used if the family of the departed is in agreement to have this done. A dance to comfort the loved ones may also be done. A prophetic dance may be done if the Lord chooses to manifest Himself in such a way.

4. Baby Dedication—A dance to celebrate life or to speak God's goodness into the life of the child and family may be done. A prophetic dance may also be done if the Holy Spirit leads.

5. Evangelistic Service—A dance concert may be sponsored by the church for the purpose of evangelism. Unsaved people who may not go to a church, *may* go to a dance concert. The dances may tell a story that reveals God's love for mankind. It may speak of Jesus' crucifixion. It may be the life of one of the disciples. It may be based on one of the books of the Bible. It may depict a personal testimony. It may deal with being set free from drugs, etc.

The dance concert may be held in a local community center, in the park, in a theater, in the church, or at the beach. It may be performed in a school or in a nursing home. These types of concerts should, for the most part, be choreographed unless otherwise directed by the Holy Spirit.

Chapter 5

Flowing Together With the Pastor, Music Leader, and Dance Leader

At that time, David began the custom of using choirs ["Chorus" is defined in the *Webster's Dictionary* as "a line of dancers" It comes from the Greek word *choros* which means, "to be a dance leader"] *in the Tabernacle to sing thanksgiving to the Lord. Asaph was the director of this choral group of priests* (1 Chronicles 16:7 TLB).

As mentioned in a previous chapter, the praise and worship dance team should start out dancing with the musicians at the beginning of the praise service. As the Father inhabits the praises of His people and the anointing comes upon the congregation, the dance leader will know whether to continue to dance or not. The Holy Spirit will then make it known to the entire praise and worship team whom He desires to manifest Himself through: the guitar player and the dancers together, or any other number of combinations. To discern this takes a good music leader and a good dance leader working together and knowing how to move in the Spirit as God directs. A good music leader will usually keep order in the song service by calling out who the Holy Spirit wants to use. It will bear witness with the dance leader and pastor.

In many churches, the pastor leads the song service because he has the oversight of the service and operates in the prophetic. Once he gets a mature music leader who can move in the prophetic, he can then release that responsibility to that leader. In some cases, the pastor flows like King David and leads the church into the prophetic.

It is good for the music leader and the dance leader to get together and practice with their teams so they can learn the flow of the Spirit as both groups flow together. The dance leader must be skilled in not only dancing, but also in moving in the prophetic. He or she must discern when God wants part of the team to sit down during a prophetic flow. The Holy Spirit may want just one dancer to dance, or two of them, or all of them, or none of them. Humility must be a part of the character of all involved so as to yield to the person or persons God chooses to use.

In our dance team, we developed eye signals so that the dancers would know by my looking at them if I wanted them to sit or to dance. We also developed signals with the pastor or music leader to know what to do without creating a distraction. Sometimes the signals had to be verbal if God wanted to do something unusual, such as telling all the men in the church to march around the sanctuary.

The congregation must be trained to understand the dancers are not there to entertain them. They are there to praise and worship God. Just as the singers may sing the same songs, the dancers may use the same steps. Just as the congregation's prayers may be the same prayers, so the dance movements may be the same until the Holy Spirit comes and takes over the service.

Should people look at the dancers while they dance? Do people look at the preacher when he preaches? Do people look at the singers or musicians when they sing or play their instruments? Sometimes. Sometimes looking at the dancers may cause you to see Jesus in them and may bring a breakthrough in your life. Sometimes closing your eyes and seeing Jesus in your mind will bring the breakthrough. It will be different each time. The Holy Spirit will lead you.

The dancer should not dance to please the congregation or to impress the pastor. They should be focused on praising God. The pastor should not select dancers to impress the visitors. He should choose dancers sent and anointed by God.

God is a God of order, yet He is also the God of liberty and creativity and spontaneity. With this in mind, let us consider the appropriate protocol concerning dancing. Would you interrupt the pastor in the middle of preaching to share a truth the Holy Spirit revealed to you as you were listening to the preaching? No. It would be inappropriate. God has a time for everything and an order for everything. Likewise, it is not appropriate for people to get up and dance during the time the praise and worship team is dancing, except at one's seat, in the back of the sanctuary, or in the aisle.

As the dancers minister unto the Lord and the anointing falls, God may want them to do a prophetic dance, a dance of warfare, etc. If, during that time, there were people other than the dance team dancing in the front of the church, it would be a hindrance to the dancers, just as it would hinder a pastor to be interrupted in the middle of preaching.

Once the prophetic flow is released from the heavenlies, the Lord may direct the dance leader or the music leader to invite the entire congregation to start dancing, at which point, people may come to the front of the church to dance.

At that time, the Lord may want a member from the congregation to do a prophetic dance, sing a song of the Lord, give a prophetic word, etc. That would be the appropriate time for members of the congregation to release all that they "hath," as in "everyone hath a song, hath a word," etc.

Always remember that God speaks from the top down and not from the bottom up. Keeping this in mind will keep you from being in rebellion like Miriam who challenged Moses and ended up getting leprosy. Wait for your praise and worship leaders to call forth the time for congregation involvement and you will be safe. If you feel you had a message and they did not give you the opportunity to bring it forth, it could be that you have the right message but the time is not yet arrived for it to be released. It could be that you are being tried like David to see if you will throw a javelin at Saul or if you will wait for your appointed time.

If you feel the leadership is in error, then pray for them. The fervent prayers of a righteous person availeth much (see Jas. 5:16). Please do not be used of the devil to bring division to the church. You may end up like Judas.

Please understand that all the Lord does in people's lives is to ultimately fulfill His plan of redemption. If you keep your eye on God's bigger plan, it will unlock your destiny and set you free from the "my ministry" syndrome that most of us have been guilty of.

Sometimes the Holy Spirit may want to use some or all the praise and worship team to bring forth a prophetic dance. There are times when the pastor or someone else will sing a prophetic song and the dance team will, at the same time, dance and interpret through body movement what is being prophesied in song. A dance leader must be very sensitive to the Holy Spirit so as not to hinder the move of God.

There are times when God will allow someone to come and dance with the dance team.

One example, an exception to the rule, the Lord brought to my remembrance was an occasion when a lady from the congregation got up to dance in the front of the congregation while the dance team was dancing. Usually this is unacceptable for reasons we spoke about previously. In this situation, however, the Lord told me not only to let her dance, but for us (the dance team) to kneel down, form a circle, and allow her to dance in the middle. The Holy Spirit showed me that the reason for doing this was to heal her from rejection. Her movements were not at all graceful, but it did not matter because the reason the Lord let her dance was to bring inner healing. So, you see, the dance leader has to be very sensitive to the Holy Spirit to keep from missing what the Holy Ghost is doing.

There have been times where people have been in the flesh and they have been asked to sit down. Discernment into the purposes of God is of vital importance. Here's a note to pastors: You can minimize hurt feelings, misunderstandings, and rebellion by knowing how to be in authority. If a prophetic word is to come forth, it will benefit the congregation if you will inform the congregation that someone has a prophetic word to be given. That will help the person who is insecure, young in the Lord, or lacks faith. He or she will then feel comfortable in releasing the prophetic utterance. It will also affirm the person and prevent the devil from tormenting them if after every prophetic word given you acknowledge it as from God. If it is soulish, you can find a tactful way to deal with it so as not to hurt the person. Of course, if it is a satanic manifestation, then you have to deal with it accordingly so as to avoid confusion and disruption of the service.

All of us should sing unto the Lord. All of us should share the gospel with the lost. All of us should dance unto the Lord. However, not all of us have been called to be in the choir. Not all of us have been called to be a pastor. Not all of us have been called to be in the ministry of dance.

The people in the ministry of dance should feel a call of God to this ministry. They must have the ability to follow the rhythm of the music. It kills the anointing when one sees a person dancing who has no rhythm. It takes away from the gracefulness and flow of the team. The dance leader has to have love, tactfulness, and creativity to use the person in another dance-related area, such as costumes, make-up, banners, etc. If a person feels led to be in a dance team but does not have the rhythm to stay in sync with the other dancers, he or she may join the banners team.

Following is a list of various dance teams that can exist in a church:

A. *Praise and Worship*

During the praise and worship portion of the service, the praise and worship dance team is the team that should dance while the singers and musicians minister unto the Lord. They are the ones who will move in the prophetic and call in the other dance teams to minister as the Holy Spirit leads.

B. *Signing*

You can have a dance team that also does signing as they dance or you can have a person signing at one side of the sanctuary while the praise and worship dance team dances. (*Signing* is when people use their hands to interpret the words being sung.)

C. *Flags*

This can be a special dance team whose members can be in their dance outfits at all services ready to be used should the Lord call for the flags. Or, the praise and worship dance team can have the flags on the side of the sanctuary ready to be used should the Holy Spirit call for flags to be used. They can do choreographed routines as the Holy Spirit leads with the approval of the leader of the dance team.

D. Pantomime

The mime dance troupe may be called on to do a prophetic dance. They may do a choreographed dance as a teaching, an edification, an exhortation, or whatever the Holy Spirit wants to portray on a certain day. They will not be used in every church service. They can also be used to travel and minister in different places as a means of evangelism.

E. Drama

The drama dance troupe may be made up of some, all, or none of the dancers in the praise and worship dance team. The drama dance team will not be used every church service. They will be used only when the Holy Spirit calls for them. They may know in advance or they may be called spontaneously. The drama dance team may also be used to travel for the purpose of evangelism.

F. Traveling

The traveling dance team is a team of evangelists whose mission is to travel to present the gospel through dance.

G. Banners

You can have a group of people assigned to carry banners as the Holy Spirit leads or they can be carried by the praise and worship dance team or by the people the Holy Spirit indicates through the channel of the dance team leader or the pastor or the music leader, as needed.

In areas of visible ministry, we need to be realistic in the limitations we have. Would you sing a solo if you could not carry a tune? It would send shivers up our spines to hear a singer trying to hit a high note when he or she sings out of tune. It is the same with dance.

On the other hand, there are people who have been called to dance and have rhythm but have not been trained in the dance. These people should be taken into the team and trained. All they need is to learn the vocabulary of dance. You don't have to be a Pavlova (a famous Russian ballerina), but you do have to have a sense of rhythm and gracefulness. The Holy Spirit will give you the anointing, and that is what will destroy the yokes as you dance.

In order to be a dancer in the house of God, you *must* be born again, baptized in the Holy Ghost, skillful in the things of the Spirit, and able to flow in the prophetic. As a dancer you must be an intercessor. Before you go to church, you must have sought the Holy Ghost in preparation to be used of God. You cannot have one foot in the world and one in God's Kingdom. It takes sacrifice, commitment, and dedication. It takes humility, obedience, and submission to the authorities God has set over you. It takes cooperation with the rest of the dance team and especially with the leadership. They have enough wars to fight. They don't need you to be used of the devil to bring strife and division.

Should children be a part of the praise and worship team? In my opinion, only children who are like Samuel and are serious and mature about the things of God should be a part of the *permanent* dance team. These children must have parents or some adult who will take the responsibility of interceding for them because they will be seriously attacked by the enemy. The singers, musicians, and dancers go ahead of the army and they are attacked first (see Psalm 68:25).

My personal belief is that children should be in training and should be allowed to participate at appointed times. I believe that they should not be in the regular praise and worship team, as cute as they may be, because they are not mature enough to know how to fight the battles. As in everything, there are exceptions to the rule, as I mentioned earlier. Those who are like Samuel should be allowed a permanent position. As I travel throughout the country, I find that Samuels are in the minority. If the teacher sees a child whom he or she feels God would want to use in the permanent praise dance team, the leader of the praise dance team should be made aware of it so he or she can be in prayer about it.

They should be given an opportunity to dance for special occasions so they will keep their interest and have something to look forward to. They should work on a choreographed dance and perhaps be allowed to present the dance once a month so they can get used to excellence.

As I said before, the singers and the dancers go ahead of the army so you had best be prepared for the attacks of the enemy. You had better be a strong soldier or you will get wiped out. But, if you keep your eyes on Jesus, He will keep you in perfect peace, and He will protect you and give you mighty testimonies of what He has done for you. When you see the victories being won, you will be glad you paid the price!

Chapter 6

How to Start a Dance Team

If your church is interested in starting a dance team, you must birth it through intercession. As you pray, the Holy Spirit will send you the vessels He has selected to fulfill His purpose. After the leadership of the church has first been in intercession, a meeting may be announced to explain the vision to the congregation concerning the dance in the church. People who feel led to be a part of the team should pray and seek the Lord for direction and should prepare their bodies by exercising or signing up for dance classes.

As I mentioned in a previous chapter, the Holy Spirit will dance through you, but you have to build a dance vocabulary for the Holy Spirit to pull out the steps. Just like you have to put the Word of God in you so the Holy Spirit can bring it to your remembrance, so you have to develop skill in the dance and at the appointed time the Lord will do the rest.

Attending a dance seminar or having someone come to your church to start your team and to train them would save you a lot of headaches. A good teacher will not only train the dancers in the physical movements but, most importantly, will train them to be skillful in the spirit realm, releasing them into the ministry by laying hands on them to impart the anointing, and prophesying over their life—giving direction concerning the ministry. It should be a person sent of God, anointed of God, and skillful in the dance and in the prophetic.

The teacher should also work with the music team to teach them how to flow together with the dance team. The teacher should be as an apostle to the dance with the call of God on their life for this ministry.

It is important to get an anointed dance minister of God who is not operating in rebellion because you don't want your team to receive the spirit of rebellion or any other spirits the person may be operating in that are not of God. What that person births in your dancers is what you will have to live with, at least until your team matures in the Lord. Don't judge by outward appearance. Seek God and He will reveal the person's heart to you.

Once you have selected your dance team, you need to appoint a leader. David appointed the Levites to minister to the Lord: "...no one except the Levites may carry it [the Ark of God], for God has chosen them for this purpose; they are to minister to Him forever" (1 Chron. 15:2 TLB).

Before we were in our mother's womb (see Jer. 1:5), God knew us and had a destiny in mind for us. Even before we are saved, I believe God has us involved in things that will prepare us for the future in God's Kingdom. When I look back at my childhood years, I see how God's hand was directing my life and how satan tried everything to keep me from preparing my life to fulfill God's purpose.

I started to take dance lessons at the age of 5. Dance was what I lived for. However, I always felt insecure. I always felt I was not as good as the other dancers. I did not take ballet lessons because I did not think I was good enough. Instead, I took modern jazz and creative dance.

When I went to college and wanted to major in dance, I was talked out of it by my college counselor. I was told there was too much competition out there in the world so I should major in health and physical education so I would be sure to get a job upon graduation. Since I did not take many sports classes during high school gym classes, I did not have the body or moves of an athlete.

When I had to sign up for all sports in college, I moved with the gracefulness of a dancer. I leaped and turned when I played basketball. They used to make fun of me because I looked like a ballerina when I played basketball instead of looking like an athlete.

Fifteen years after graduating from college, I became born again. I gave up dancing because I thought God did not want anything to do with dance. I did not mind giving it up because I was so in love with the Lord that I wanted to do only what pleased Him.

One day, the Holy Spirit came upon me while I was in church and told me to get up and dance. I was disobedient because I thought people were not supposed to dance in church. After looking into the Scriptures, I realized I was wrong. The next time I felt that anointing I was obedient and it was the greatest experience I had ever had in feeling the manifested presence of God.

It was seven months to a year before I joined the church to which I now belong. The church I had been a member of previously did not believe in the dance. I felt like I went to hell and back as a result of the persecutions I experienced there. However, God used that time to work on my character. The insecurity and rejection I had felt as a child helped to prepare me for the rejection and false accusations I faced as I entered into the ministry of dance. After I had been a member of the church for several months and I had been proven by the leadership of the church, the Lord told my pastor to ordain me as the leader of the dance team.

God does not believe in democracy in the Church. He appoints whom He chooses. The reason many churches are in trouble and there is no glory of God manifested in the midst of the sanctuary is because men politic and vote on whom the leadership should be.

In our church, the leadership seeks the Lord for His choice of leaders. We fast and pray until God brings the direction and points His finger of choice. God confirms it through His prophets. We usually have ministers from other congregations who prophesy the word of the Lord over the people to be ordained, and the Lord always confirms His word in the midst of the congregation.

In selecting a person to lead the dance team, the first and most important consideration, as mentioned earlier, is God's election. Other considerations to see if the person is ready to answer the call are:

1. Has the person been proven faithful in the church?

2. Does the person have the heart of a servant or are they serving to be noticed and to gain a position? God will reveal this to the leadership if they will seek the Lord.

3. Does the person share the vision of the house and do they have the spirit of the leader? If they do not, they will seek to establish their own vision and will bring division.

4. Is the person skillful in the things of God and especially in the area they will be leading in? Skill does not mean, in the case of dance, being a "Pavlova." You can have a person who is a great dancer but is not mature in the realm of the Spirit and thus cannot be a father or mother to the team, spiritually speaking. Thus, they are not able to birth more children into the team. When trouble comes, they will not know how to deal with it wisely. Therefore, a combination of both physical and spiritual maturity is necessary to lead a dance team.

We are told in the New Testament to come in boldly to the throne of God, as compared to the Old Testament when only the high priest could go into the holiest of holies. But, although we as born-again believers can come boldly to the throne of God and God hears our prayers even before we ask Him, we cannot always hear from God immediately. Our soul sometimes gets in the way. Sometimes there is war in the heavenlies and it takes pressing in to get the breakthrough to hear what God is saying.

I believe a dancer should be a person who knows how to press in until the breakthrough comes. A dancer should have a burden for intercession. A dancer should have God's purpose and the church's purpose in mind, not his or her own agenda that takes away from the vision of the church. A dancer should know how to be under authority to best promote the Kingdom of God. A dancer should be one who promotes unity in the Body of Christ. A dancer is one who is willing to learn. If he or she is an excellent dancer, he or she should be willing to help the leader in any way possible. (The person who is the best dancer may not be the one God chooses to use as a leader.) Dancers should contribute their talents to help the leader fulfill his or her responsibility to the local church as he or she leads the dance team.

For example, when I was leading the dance team in our church, we had a woman who was very creative and sewed excellently. She was one of the dancers, and her contribution to the team was sewing banners, head pieces, and other accessories.

We had another dancer who trained with a professional dance team. She was the most talented dancer in our team, so I gave her the most difficult choreographed parts in the dance routines. She also helped with the choreography and with advanced dance techniques and exercise during rehearsal.

One of the most important contributions to the team was provided by the assistant leader. There were many times when I would have to travel and she took over for me. She was such a reliable person and had such a loving disposition that I felt peace knowing all would be well in my absence. She had the heart of a servant and was never in competition with me. Since the writing of this book, she has become the leader because I am an ordained minister and travel extensively.

If dancers have the reverential fear of God and understand that it is God's Kingdom and not theirs, they will not be fighting for position like the world. Those who fight for position are not skillful in the things of God, and their pride opens them up to be used of satan to bring strife and division to the team. They operate under a spirit of rebellion, which opens them up to witchcraft and a Jezebel spirit.

In one of the books my pastor wrote, the Lord gave him a prophecy that there would be those in the Body of Christ who, like the prodigal son, would want their inheritance now but would then come back to the Father like the prodigal son. I guess it is human nature to want to go ahead of our time. God will allow it, but it will be costly because, like the prodigal son, the Father will be hurt as well as the son during that period of rebellion.

The good thing about it is that what the devil intends for evil, God turns to good. So, leaders, be encouraged. Your prodigal sons will come home. During their absence, you will have learned how to love them with the unconditional love of a father. You will have become like Jesus who loved Judas even though He knew Judas would betray Him.

One of my favorite teachings from my mentor is that every church has a Judas who will betray the leader. Every church has a Thomas who will doubt. Every church has a Peter who will deny you. Each one will be used by God to sandpaper the leader to form him or her into the image of Jesus, since the character of Christ is what we hope to develop in our lives. When these things happen in your team, thank the Lord and ask Him to show you what part of your character He is wanting to change to make you more like Him.

Chapter 7

Technical Aspects of Dance

When I first started dancing, I did not know what my boundaries were as I led the dance team, so I always asked the pastor's permission before I did anything. As we learned to work together, he gave me the liberty to move as I felt led of the Holy Spirit. That gave me a sense of security and confidence that allowed me to move freely as the Holy Spirit led.

As I mentioned in an earlier chapter, our praise and worship team danced during the praise and worship service. When the prophetic was released, we danced and interpreted what was being prophesied. If the Holy Spirit did not want us to do so, we sat down. If I, as a leader, missed it and sat down but the pastor wanted us to interpret the prophetic in dance, he gave me eye signals to come back to dance or he verbally called the dance team or an individual to dance. If the Lord led me to do something that seemed out of the ordinary, I would go to the pastor and tell him what I believed the Lord wanted us to do and He would give me the okay or tell me not to do it until a later time or not at all.

Often, the dancers can only go as high as the musicians take them. It is the music that pulls the creativity and the anointing out of the dancer. If the musicians are off, the dancers will have difficulty dancing. They will have to dance by faith and do warfare for the musicians so they can get the breakthrough.

One of the things the Lord has taught me since I started dancing unto the Lord is to offer the sacrifice of praise until it is totally consumed. Many churches have not seen the miracles of God because they have a "popcorn" service. They start in the outer court and then jump into the holy of holies, then to the holy place, then to the outer court, and so on. In other words, they sing a song of thanksgiving, then go into a song of worship (or so they think), then they sing a song of war, then a song of praise, and there is no rhyme or reason to the order of their song selection.

God has told us how to approach Him. He said enter into His gates with *thanksgiving* and into His courts with *praise*. Notice He did not tell us that the next thing to do is worship. That is because God initiates worship as an answer to our thanksgiving and praise, as was mentioned in an earlier chapter.

The praise service should be like a circle. First we thank God, then we praise Him until He invites us into worship. I do not want to get legalistic about the order of praise, but in church services that follow the order of God, I have never seen the people disappointed. God always shows up. If we don't allow the sacrifice of praise to be totally consumed because of time, we will be missing out on the manifested presence of the glory of God. This is what many of us are guilty of today. We are on our time, and the Holy Spirit has to step aside for us to fulfill our plans. This is the reason we do not see salvations, healings, deliverances, and other divine manifestations. We know these things can happen on a daily basis as we go out into the highways and byways. However, salvations, healings, and deliverances happen through vessels who have spent time in their prayer closet with God and who have spent time praising God. They happen through vessels whose temples are filled with the glory of God because they are connected to God through prayer, praise, and adoration.

Another area of consideration for the praise department is the words of the songs. The power of life and death is in our tongue. Let us sing songs that bring life and not death. Let us sing more *to* God. It is fine to sing *about* God, but it is better to sing *to* God. For example, a husband may say to a friend, "I have a great wife. I really love her." The wife feels good about having her husband brag about her. However, the feeling is more intense if the husband tells his wife in front of their friends, "Honey, you are a great wife. I love you very much." It is more personal and more heartwarming to the wife. So, when we sing *to* God instead of singing *about* God, it touches God's heart in a greater way.

Another area to consider is the signaling between the dance leader and the dancers. As the dance leader has signals he or she uses to help him or her flow with the music leader and with the pastor, he or she must also have signals to flow with the other dancers. When I was the leader of the dance team in our church, we had five dancers dancing during each service. We usually started out in a "V" formation. I would form the bottom part of the "V" so the dancers could see me. Behind me would be two dancers on either side of me. Behind them would be two dancers on either side. As we danced, they followed what I did.

This was usually not choreographed because when we first started we did not have a place available for us to practice. Our church started out in a rented hotel ballroom, and the dancers came from as far as one and a half to two hours away from where the church met. Thus, we did not have the opportunity to get together for practice. The Lord anointed us to work together spontaneously. The team had no idea what my next move was going to be, yet they followed me as

I moved. It looked so organized that people would ask us how long we practiced to make it look so good. They were shocked when we told them we had not practiced. God just did it through us. I believe the Lord allowed us to not have room to practice because He wanted us to learn to dance spontaneously at His leading so we would not get into a choreographed mode.

As we went along, we learned hand signals. I would assign a leader from each twosome. At a point in the dance when I felt the Holy Spirit telling me to add variety to the dance moves I would so signal. If I wanted us to form a circle, I would circle my index finger. That meant to prepare to go into a circle. As we did the circle, I would softly speak the next instruction to them. I might then tell them to march into a line or to march around the room. Whatever we did, we always ended back in the starting position ready for the next signal.

Each team of two girls had a leader. The reason for this was to add variety to the dance routine. It is sort of like having altos, sopranos, tenors, and basses in a choir for melody, harmony, and variety in tone.

When it was time to have each team of two do something different than what I was doing, I would point to the leaders. That meant that immediately they were now in charge of making up their own steps. The leaders would make up a step and the second girl would follow. Each team of two would do their own steps, and I would do my own steps that would blend in with what they were doing. I also gave them instructions prior to starting the praise service. If one team was doing movements that were traveling upward movements, the other team should do stationary lower movements to add dimension and depth to the dance.

Another technique we used to add creativity and to express what the Lord wanted to say through the dance or what we wanted to say to the Lord through the dance was a solo. We would have the dance team move toward the back of the platform while one of the dancers would do a solo. While the dancer was doing the solo, if the dance was a slow dance, we did soft, gentle arm movements in the background. If the dance was a percussive dance, we might stomp our feet or clap our hands.

Perhaps the Lord will give you other ways of accomplishing what we accomplished. He is a God of creativity and there is no limit to what He can do through us and for us. I just wanted to give the above examples for those who have not yet started their dance teams and for those who are still seeking the pattern to follow concerning dance in the house of God.

Thus far, we have looked at the spiritual aspect of dance and at how to move with the dance leader and the praise team. Now we are going to take a closer look at the skeleton and muscles of the dance—the technical aspects.

A. **Dance Movement**: The following is a list of various dance movement techniques:
   1. Unison—dancers can dance in unison, as all dance alike.
   2. Opposition—to add interest to a dance or to express difference, turmoil, or opposition, dancers may move in steps that are in opposition to the other part of the dance team.
   3. Succession—to create variety or emphasize a point, dancers may repeat the same movement in succession or, in other words, one after the other.

B. **Focus**: Focus is another dimension of dance.
   1. Looking up can mean hope, expectation, pride, searching.
   2. Looking away can mean rejection, denial, no, anger.

3. Looking down can mean sorrow, humility, inferiority, shame, looking for something.

C. **Quality of Movement**
   1. Pendular movement—a free swinging movement at the torso, at the knee, at the elbow. It creates a feeling of openness, naturalness, and freedom.
   2. Sustained movement—a steady, equalized release of energy with no interruption. The lifting of the leg in a slow, even motion is a good example. Another example is the motion of stretching an elastic band in a slow, even motion. It could be used to express beauty, strength, patience, gracefulness, love, etc.
   3. Percussive movement—a strong, sharp, aggressive movement such as dodging, throwing, jumping, or kicking. It has much force and a quick contraction. This can be used to express anger, war, rebellion, a troop of soldiers marching, etc.
   4. Vibratory movement—a quivering or shaking, pulsating movement. This can be used to express fear, sickness, strength, glory, or sun rays.
   5. Collapse—the absence of any tension, a controlled fall, a complete relaxation of the entire body or of a particular body part. This can be used to express having received a hit, death, tiredness, giving up, etc.

D. **Dance Movement Breakdown**
   1. Jump—to spring, to bounce, to go over, to recoil, to spring upon, to pounce upon, to change abruptly, to advance.
   2. Slide—to glide, to move smoothly over a surface while keeping continuous contact with the floor. One foot moves to the side, to the front, or to the back and the other foot comes to meet it in a series of repetitions.

3. Walk—to advance in a certain direction by placing one foot in front of the other. One can change the level of the walk by bending knees, by walking on toes, or by a combination of both. One can walk frontward, sideways, or backward.

4. Leap—to move off the ground with a spring of the legs.

5. Stag Leap—to leap as a deer by kicking forward with the forward leg and then bending that same leg and stretching the rear leg back to give the move a deer-leap appearance.

6. Fall—to come down from an erect position while giving in to gravity. One can fall to the side, front, back, or straight down.

7. Run—to move swiftly on foot with both feet leaving the ground during each stride. One can run forward, backward, or at a diagonal.

8. Sit—to assume a position with the body resting on the buttocks. One can sit up straight, in a slouched position, or leaning against an object.

9. Turn—to move around a center or axis, also to revolve or rotate.

10. Contract—to draw together or shrink. An example of this would be to bend the body at the waist and bring chest to knees.

11. Kick—to strike out with the foot. One can kick forward, backward, or sideways.

12. Push—to press against someone or something forcibly in order to move oneself or to move someone else.

13. Swing—to move freely back and forth in an arch as if suspended. One can swing the arms, legs, torso, or head.

14. Bend—to bring the upper torso down to meet the legs; to bring the upper torso sideways towards the lower torso; to bend at the joints to bring a body part closer to another body part.
15. Reach—to stretch out a body part.
16. Shake—to move with short quick movements; to tremble. One can shake the hands, arms, legs, head, and torso.
17. Shiver—to shake as if from being cold or frightened. The movements in shivering are quicker than the movements in shaking.

(Note: The above definitions are my own definitions as I have tried to describe each dance movement. I have used the *Webster's II New Riverside Dictionary* for assistance.)

E. **Floor Pattern**—God is a creative God. He is an exciting God. He is a God of variety. In praising and worshiping Him, we must allow the Holy Spirit to give us creativity in the patterns we create while dancing. Using a variety of floor patterns in a dance composition will add variety and dimension to the dance, consider the following:

1. Line—a line can be used for marching, for unity, for strength, etc.
2. Diagonal—a diagonal line can be used to indicate progression.
3. Circle—a circle can be used to indicate strength, protection, unity, entrapment, etc.
4. "V"—a "V" pattern may be used to indicate victory, strength, etc.
5. Scattered Formation—a scattered formation may be used to indicate confusion, individuality, a crowd scene, diversity, etc.

These floor patterns may be used in various combinations to tell a story or to more adequately express an idea as they combine with proper dance movements.

F. **Level**—As we read the Word of God, each word we read expresses a certain idea. When Jesus spoke certain parables, He then had to turn to the disciples to explain the parables. Certain principles the disciples understood, and other things had to be explained to them. Likewise, in dancing before the Lord, the movements used and the levels used in the dance have a certain meaning. Sometimes an explanation of the dance must be given so the congregation can understand what the dancers are expressing. At other times, the Holy Spirit will supernaturally reveal to the congregation what the dancers are expressing.

Listed below are a few examples of what different levels mean to a dancer or to the congregation that is partaking in receiving a blessing from the Lord through the dance ministry. Most importantly, what is the dancer saying to God as he or she worships Him in the dance?

1. Lying down on the floor—This position could be used to express total surrender to God or to another being. It could also mean awe of God, or be used to show death, sleeping, tiredness, or defeat. It also means submission.
2. Kneeling—This position could express prayerfulness, begging, repentance, worship, humility, etc.
3. Sitting—This position could express rest, sitting at someone's feet, pondering a situation, giving up, etc.
4. Standing—This position could express praise, confidence, strength, victory, etc.
5. Jumping—This position could express rejoicing, victory, frustration, force, warfare, etc.

G. **Suggested Exercises**

Scripture states that exercise profits little. However, in today's sedentary society where everything is instant and our body seldom gets exercised in our daily jobs, our body requires exercise to keep functioning properly. Those called into the ministry of dance need to practice and keep their bodies fit. Just as a musician practices and keeps his instrument tuned, so a dancer must practice to achieve as high a degree of excellence as he or she is capable of achieving. Coordination, agility, flexibility, and stamina can only be achieved through practice on a regular basis.

There have been times in our church services when the Holy Spirit desired to prophesy through the dance team or to do spiritual warfare through the dance team. One such occurrence lasted for two hours. Had our bodies not been in shape, it would have been difficult to flow with the Holy Spirit because our tiredness would have hindered our being in tune with what the Holy Spirit was trying to accomplish. (This warfare anointing was an outpouring of waves of the Holy Spirit bringing a refreshing, which had been badly needed, to the local church body.)

The following is a list of suggested exercises (consult your physician before doing these exercises):

1. Ankle Rotation—Stand with feet shoulder width apart. Press on the ball of the right foot and in circular motion, rotate the ankle to the outside 8 times. Now rotate the same foot to the inside 8 times. Repeat with left foot. It is important to start with ankle warm-ups to avoid ankle injuries.

2. Run in Place—Run in place for 50 counts, bringing knees up to waist level. This exercise will develop endurance and should be done rapidly. It also helps prepare the body for exercising by getting an increase of blood flow to all body parts.

3. Slide—Slide to the right to the count of 4. Start by bringing the right foot to the right side (starting with

feet shoulder width apart). Next, have the left foot move to meet the right foot. Continue to repeat this pattern until you reach the opposite side of the room. Then repeat in the opposite direction beginning with the left foot. Repeat entire set 4 times.

4. Walk—Walk forward with knees *slightly* bent in a semi-crouch position. Reach out in front of you with the opposite hand of the foot that is forward. Repeat to count of 4.

   Alternate the above walk with the following: Walk forward while on your toes and reach to the ceiling with your hands. Knees will be straight except for a slight bend when switching feet.

   Combine the above two walks to the count of: down—2, 3, 4; up—2, 3, 4. Repeat for the length of the floor, then start over from that side of the room back to where you started.

5. Leg Lifts—Find a partner, then face each other and stand side to side. Hold on to each other for support by placing your right hand on the other person's shoulder. This will be your support position for the next set of exercises.

   a. Lift right leg to the front to the count of 4, then lower it to the count of 4. Repeat set 4 times.

   b. Repeat the above procedure but bring the right leg to the side instead of to the front.

   c. Repeat the above procedure but bring the right leg to the back.

   d. Repeat a, b, and c with the left leg.

   This exercise may be used to strengthen muscles on the upper leg so as to develop the ability to hold the leg in a controlled position for a length of time.

e. Repeat all the steps, but instead of bringing the leg up in a controlled sequence of 4 counts, bring the leg up to a quick count of 1 and down to the count of "and." Example: "1 and, 2 and, 3 and, 4 and ...."

The purpose of this exercise is to stretch the muscles in the upper leg to give them flexibility and strength.

6. Toe Touching—Stand up straight with arms down by your sides. On the count of 1, bring hands up and reach towards the ceiling. On the count of 2, place your hands on your hips. On the count of 3, touch the floor with your hands. Note: go as far down as you can without bending your knees. If you cannot touch the floor, it's okay. Keep exercising until your flexibility increases with exercises.

On the count of 4, come back up to a standing position and place your hands on your hips to finish one set. Repeat the entire exercise 10 times. Then stay down and touch your toes for 10 counts.

7. Side Bends—Stand with feet shoulder distance apart. Place left hand on hip and right arm upward toward the ceiling. Now bend to the left. Pulse 8 times then alternate arms and do the same thing but to the opposite side. Repeat this sequence but instead of pulsing 8 times, pulse 4 times on the next sequence, then 2 times, then once to each side. Each of the above sequences should be repeated a total of 4 times each.

8. Curl-Ups—Lay down on your back and bend your knees. Place feet on the floor shoulder width apart. Place arms straight over head. Starting with your arms, slowly curl up to a sitting position. Then continue by bringing your arms between your knees and continue forward until your hands touch the floor in

front of you. Slowly uncurl and start going back down to the floor to starting position. This exercise will tighten your stomach muscles. Start out by doing 20 and add 5 each day until you are doing 40 curl ups per day. This exercise will improve your posture by tightening your abdominal muscles.

9. Bent Knee Push-Ups—Bend your legs so that the fatty part of the upper knee is on the floor (never do this on your patella or knee bone). Place hands on the floor in front of you. Now bend the elbows and touch the floor slightly with your chin. Keep torso straight so that hips are in line with the rest of the body. Now come back up to starting position. Start with 10 and add 2 per day until you can do 20 per day. This exercise will strengthen your upper arm and pectoral (chest) muscles.

10. Leg Stretches—Sit on floor with legs out to the sides as far as they can stretch. Bend at the hips and reach out to the right with opposite arm to touch the right foot. Pulse 8 times to the right then 8 times to the center, then 8 times to the left. Repeat the entire sequence, but pulse only 4 times. Repeat the entire sequence, but pulse only 2 times. This exercise will increase your flexibility in the muscles of the inner thigh and behind your leg.

The exercises listed above are very basic exercises. There are many other exercises you can do to maintain a strong and flexible body.

Other exercises include:
1. Neck Exercises
2. Arm Exercises
3. Splits
4. Back Bends

H. **Suggested Dance Attire**

In the Book of Revelation, we are told that all kindred and nations will worship the Lord in Heaven. Scripture admonishes us to pray that God's will be done on earth as it is in Heaven. In evangelizing, Americans have sometimes missed it. We have tried to preach the Good News in other countries, but we have brought with us the music we are accustomed to. We have Americanized the gospel. I believe we will have better success if we minister to people in the costume and music rhythm with which they are familiar.

In choosing our costumes, we need to take into consideration the nationality of the people we will be ministering to. When traveling for evangelization, we also need to involve the natives so they can feel a part of the worship. We need to learn some of their customs from them. Paul the Apostle said he made himself like the people he was with for the sake of winning them to Christ. It does not mean we bring paganism into our dance. It means that we maintain our biblical purity while incorporating that which is not against the Word of God.

Dance outfits should be modest. Women should (a) not wear low-cut dresses that would expose the chest when bowing down, (b) wear proper culottes under their dresses so as not to offend anyone when doing turns or leaps, and (c) wear proper athletic support bras so as not to attract attention to the chest when bouncing around. Men should wear a top that is long enough to cover hips so as not to attract attention to their private parts.

In everything, use wisdom. Avoid anything that would provoke sexual arousal. In dancing, watch your hip movements so as not to make sexually suggestive movements. Remember, you are not in Hollywood or in the Rockettes. God is holy so be ye holy inwardly and outwardly.

I pray this book has been a blessing unto you. May the wind of the Holy Spirit fall on you as you dance into the anointing.

Bibliography

Allison, Lora. *Celebration, Banners, Dance and Holiness in Worship*. New Wilmington, PA: Son Rise Publications and Distribution, 1987.

Conner, Kevin, Jr. *The Tabernacle of David*. Portland, OR: Bible Temple-Conner Publications, 1976.

Conner, Kevin, Jr. *The Tabernacle of Moses*. Portland, OR: Bible Temple-Conner Publications, 1975.

Hibbert, Mike & Viv. *Music Ministry*. Lewiston, NY: Scriptures in Song, 1982.

Jordan, E. Bernard. *Prophets of God's Kingdom*. Brooklyn, NY: Zoe Ministries, 1988.

Jordan, E. Bernard. *School of the Prophets*. Brooklyn, NY: Zoe Ministries, 1989.

Law, Terry. *The Power of Praise and Worship*. Tulsa, OK: Victory House Publishers, 1985.

Lockhart, Aileene. *Modern Dance Building and Teaching Lessons*. Dubuque, IA: W.M.C. Brown Co. Publishers, 1957.

Roberts, Debbie. *Rejoice: A Biblical Study of the Dance*. Little Rock, AR: Revival Press, 1985.

Thomas, Annabel. *Ballet & Dance.* Tulsa, OK: EDC Publishing, 1987.

Wright, Marilyn. *Dance Horizons.* Fresno, CA: Valley Bible Center Publications, 1987.

Prayer of Salvation

Note: It is not enough to go to church. At some point in our lives we need to make Jesus the Lord of our lives. If you have never done this, then pray this prayer:

Jesus, I believe You died for me and then rose from the dead. I believe You are the Son of God and You are God. I believe You were born of the virgin Mary, conceived by the Holy Spirit.

I confess I am a sinner, and I ask Your forgiveness for all my sins. I renounce every work of darkness from my life. I receive Your forgiveness. Now Jesus, come live in my heart and be the Lord of my life. Fill me with the Holy Spirit and give me my heavenly prayer language.

*Thank You that my name is now written in the Lamb's book of life. I am from this day on a new creation in Christ Jesus. Old things are passed away and all things are made new in my life. **All** my sins have been forgiven and I am starting a new life in You.*

Now tell someone the good news!

John 3:16-18; Romans 10:9-12; Luke 1:26-56; 1 Corinthians 14:2-5; John 14:6-29

About the Author

Prophetess Aimee Verduzco Kovacs was born in Texas. From the time she was a child dance was in her heart. Her first dance recital took place when she was five years old. Maria Luisa M. Ballas was her first mentor in the dance.

Prophetess Aimee graduated from the University of Texas with a Bachelor of Science degree. She moved to New Jersey where she met the Lord at home as she prayed for God to heal her from a tumor. This healing was the first miracle she experienced from God. Since then she has lived a life of faith and trust in God. Among many of the other miracles God has done for her are the healing of her marriage after a 15-month separation, a $10,000 miracle, healing from hypoglycemia, a second home in a warm weather climate, and many other miracles.

Prophetess Aimee is an ordained minister and also holds a Master of Biblical Counseling degree, a Doctor of Ministry in Dance, and a Doctor of Philosophy in Religion.

Prophetess Aimee has danced at the United Nations, Jerusalem, Mexico, and throughout the United States. God uses Aimee not only in the area of dance, but also in the area of marriage healing and in teaching about the complete person God created us to be—spirit, soul, and body. God has done many signs and wonders through her laying on of hands. People have been healed from cancer, financial miracles have taken place, and the prophetic word she has spoken over persons lives have set them free. God uses her to lay hands and impart the psalmist and prophetic anointing on those vessels God wants to release in those areas.

Like Queen Esther, God opened doors for Aimee to minister to the lost through having her selected to be Mrs. West Long Branch 1996. She has also been in the Mrs. New Jersey America Pageant and will be in the Mrs. New Jersey International Pageant this summer (1996). Like Queen Esther, she did not seek these titles. God opened the door and sent people her way to seek her participation in these pageants. God loves the lost and will send us their way to bring the message of salvation.

Prophetess Aimee is a cheerleader to the Body of Christ. She is full of laughter and joy. In her view, nothing is too hard for God. She lives with her husband Jim and their son Brandon. Together, Jim and Aimee have seven children and four grandchildren.

For speaking engagements, book orders, or for more information on World Wide Dominion Dancers, please write to:

Aimee Kovacs, Ph.D.

or

Kingdom Glory, Inc.

or

World Wide Dominion Dancers
P.O. Box 40
West Long Branch, New Jersey 07764